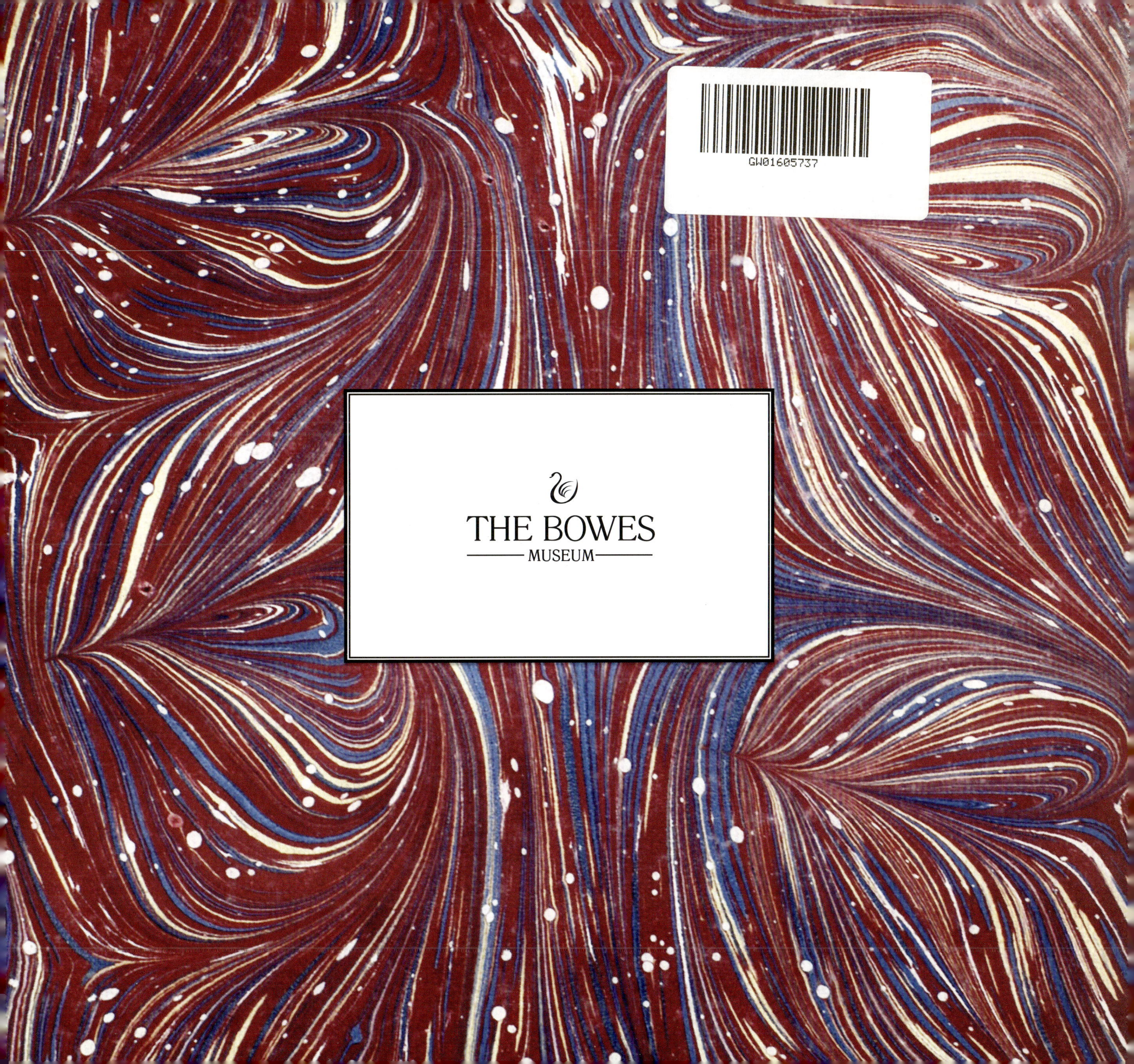
GW01605737
THE BOWES
MUSEUM

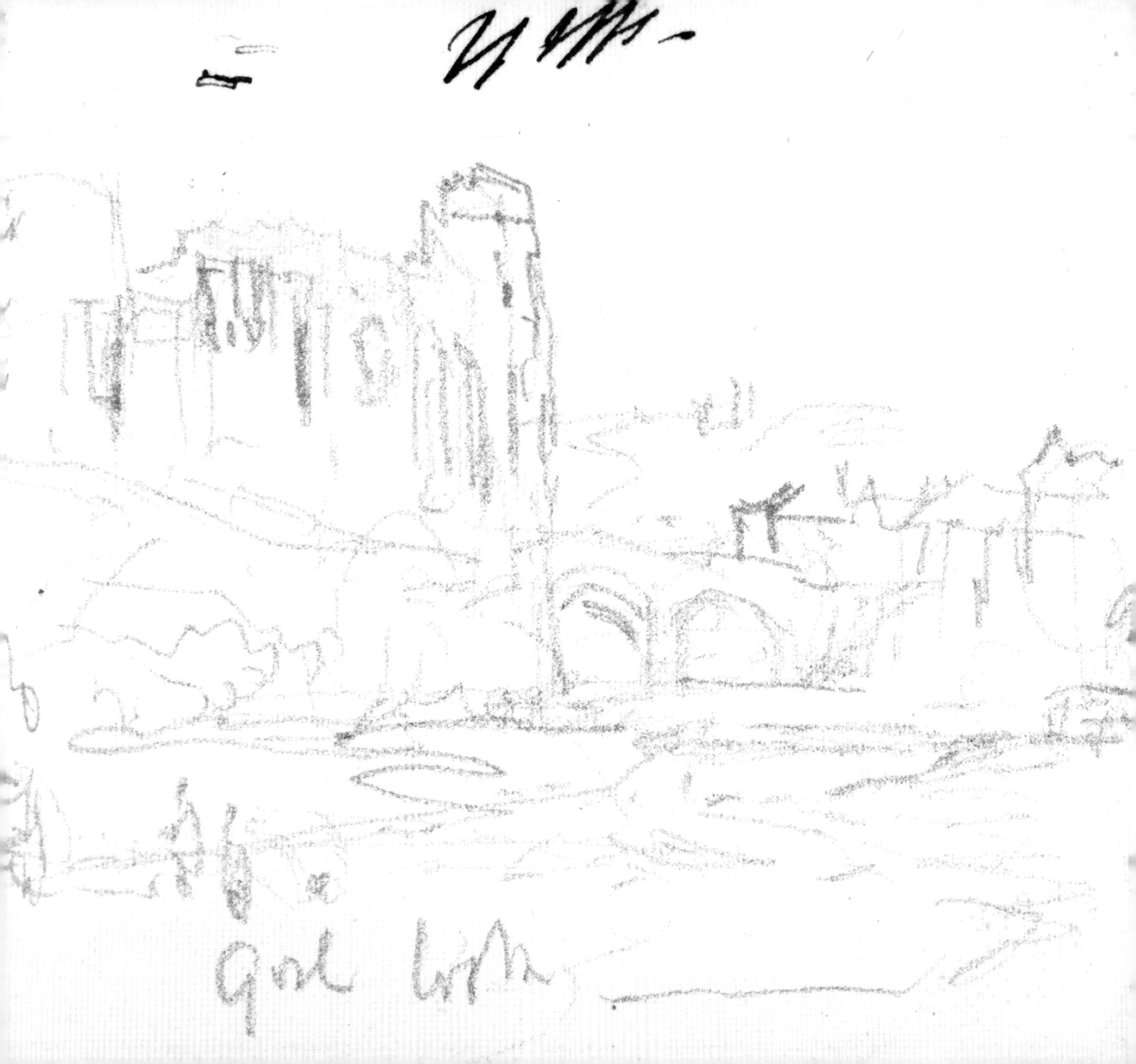

Joseph Mallord William Turner

TOURS OF DURHAM

and

RICHMONDSHIRE

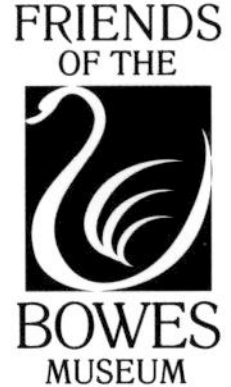

© The Bowes Museum 2006

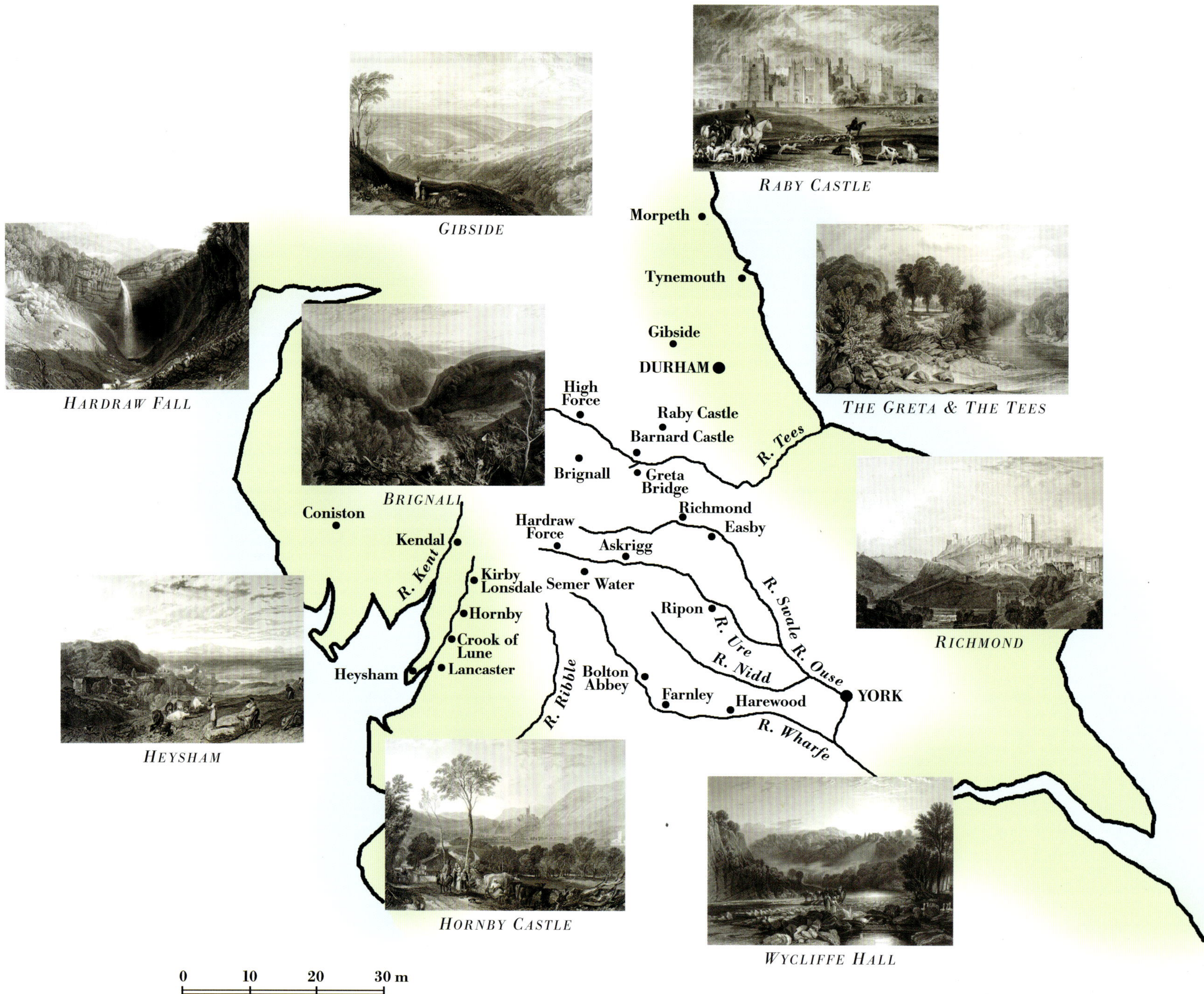

Raby Castle

Gibside

Hardraw Fall

The Greta & The Tees

Brignall

Richmond

Heysham

Hornby Castle

Wycliffe Hall

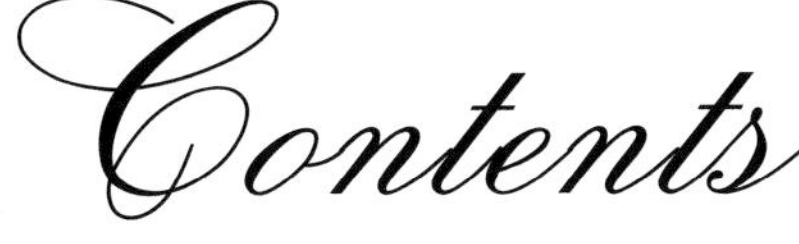

Chairman's Preface

IT IS WITH EXCITEMENT that I introduce this catalogue specially written and compiled to accompany *Turner: Tours of Durham and Richmondshire* at The Bowes Museum. The Museum is the proud owner of two of J. M. W. Turner's watercolours of the region, *Gibside from the North* and *Gibside, County Durham, The Seat of the Earl of Strathmore*, as well as engravings. The images of Gibside were commissioned in 1817 by the 10th Earl of Strathmore, the father of John Bowes, founder of The Bowes Museum along with his wife Joséphine

John Bowes, a wealthy businessman, was the illegitimate son of the Earl, benefiting from financial inheritance but not a title. In 1847 he moved to Paris and met Joséphine Coffin-Chevallier, an actress who became his wife. Their shared love of art led to the creation of a world-class museum in Teesdale, the place of John's birth. This vision is what The Bowes Museum is today; a magnificent building that is home to the most outstanding collection of European fine and decorative arts in the North of England.

It is most appropriate that this selection of works by Turner of scenes across the North of England has been brought together by The Bowes Museum. In particular his depiction of Barnard Castle itself which has never before been on display here in the County Durham market town of Barnard Castle. The exhibition has grown bigger than its title, with images from further afield, including Turner's watercolours of *Brinkburn Priory, Northumberland* and *Lancaster Sands*.

The full scope of the exhibition is recorded in this catalogue, which also contains new research on Turner's technique and use of paint. All in all it is a fascinating read through some of the tours of an artist whom many regard as Britain's greatest.

The Bowes Museum's exhibition programme, alongside its permanent collections, continues to delight and surprise. The independent Trust which governs the Museum has embarked on a series of improvements and restoration which when complete will enhance further The Bowes Museum's ability to display and interpret the fine and decorative arts. I trust you enjoy this exploration of Turner's tours of the North of England and I thank all our many supporters who journey with us to modernise and fulfil the vision of John and Joséphine Bowes.

Viscount Eccles

Chairman, Board of Trustees
The Bowes Museum

Opposite

J. M. W. Turner

(1775 – 1851)

Barnard Castle

circa 1825

Watercolour on paper

Yale Center for British Art,
Paul Mellon Center

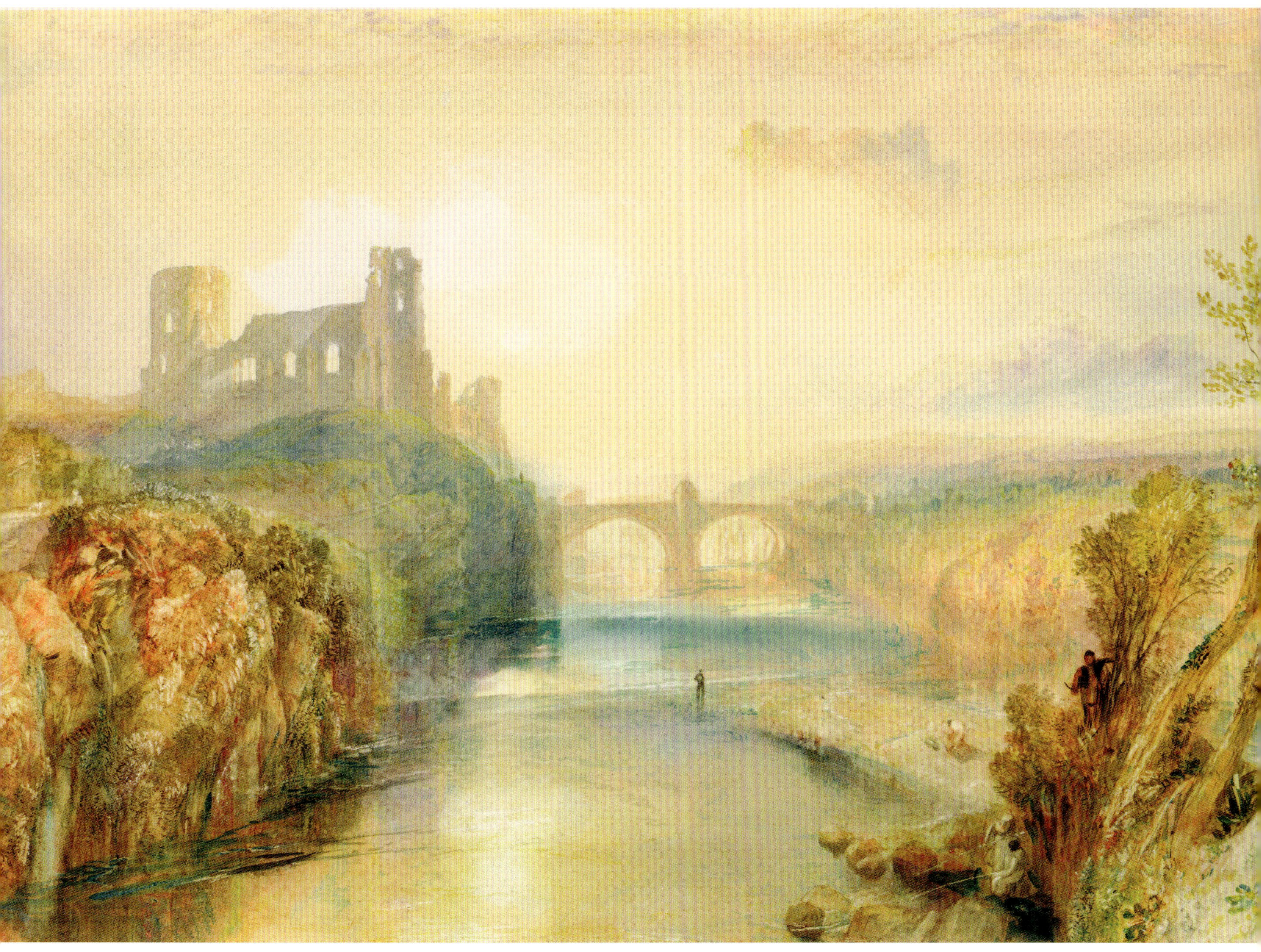

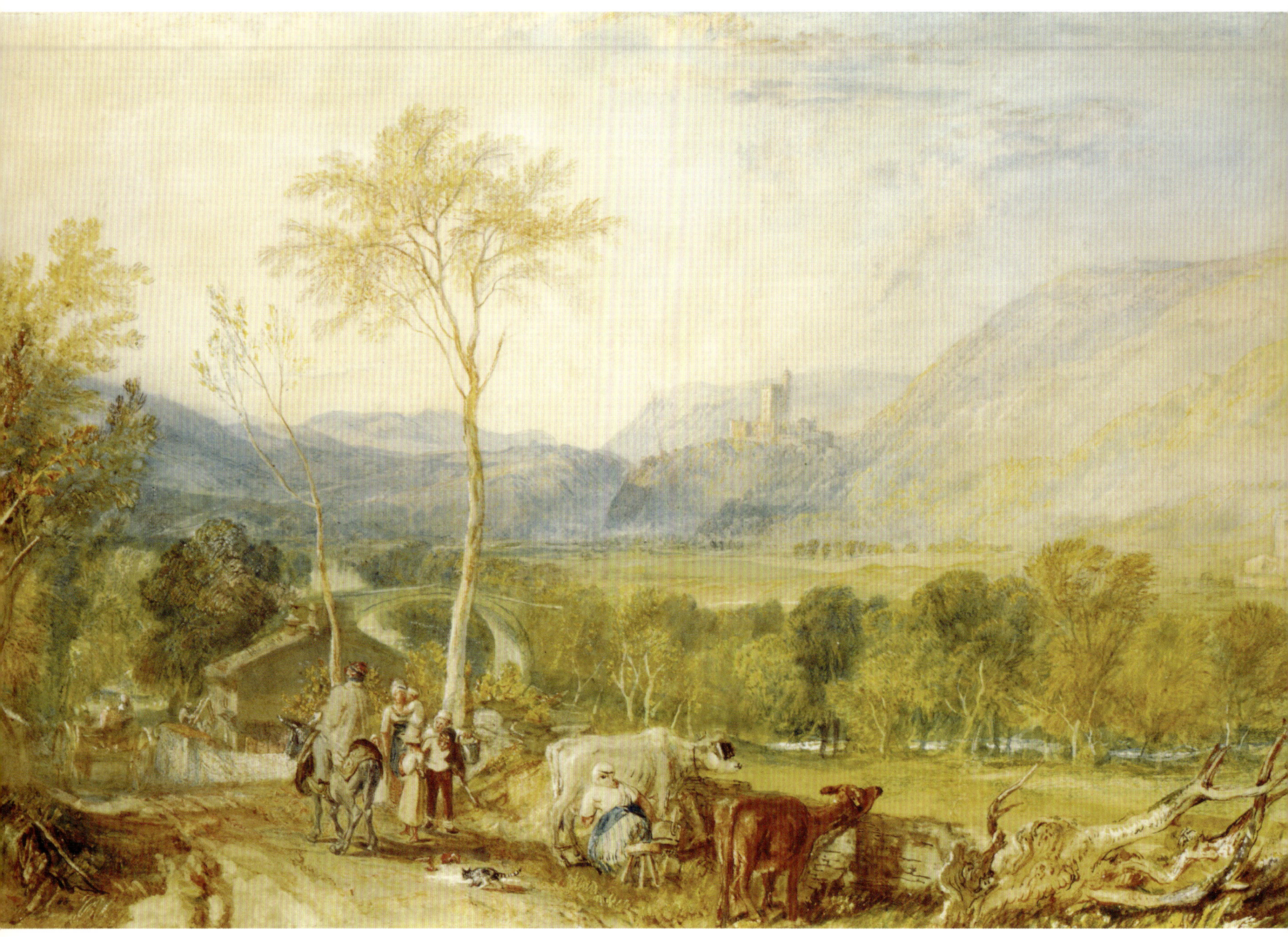

Opposite

J. M. W. Turner

Hornby Castle from Tatham Church

circa 1818

Watercolour on paper

Victoria & Albert Museum, given by John Sheepshanks

Director's Foreword *and* Acknowledgements

TURNER EXPLORED THE LANDSCAPE OF TEESDALE AROUND THE BOWES MUSEUM, on a number of occasions. Perhaps the most important trip was during the summer of 1816, following his commission form the London publisher Longman & Co., to produce finished watercolours to be used by engravers to reproduce in *An History of Richmondshire*. The trip was blighted by atrocious weather, causing Turner to complain, 'weather miserably wet; I shall be web-footed like a drake...' Despite the awful conditions, Turner went on to produce images of Northern England that influence our appreciation of its landscape even today.

This exhibition charts Turner's fascination with our region and has involved the efforts and enthusiasm of a wide range of individuals and institutions. Particular thanks for their contribution go to Emma House, Michael Rudd and Paul Clark for researching and writing the catalogue. I am also grateful to Vivien Reid, Vincent Shawcross and Mark Vallack for their practical skills in mounting the exhibition. I would also like to thank the many curators and registrars who have assisted with the organisation of loans: Anthony Griffiths, Kim Sloan and Janice Reading at the British Museum, Matthew Clough at University of Liverpool Art Gallery and Collections, Corinne Miller at Leeds City Art Gallery, Ann Chumbley of Sheffield Galleries & Museums Trust, Fiona Salvesen at Bolton Museums and Art Gallery, Jennifer Gill of Durham County Record Office, The Earl of Strathmore & Kinghorne, Sabrina Shim and Geraldine Glynn at the Ashmolean Museum, Oxford, Caroline Bacon of Cecil Higgins Art Gallery, Varshali Patel at Birmingham Museums & Art Gallery, Liz Woods and Thyrza Smith at The Fitzwilliam Museum, Cambridge, Edwina Mulvany of the Royal Academy of Arts, London, Catherine Clement at Tate, Godfrey Burke of National Museums Liverpool, Charles Nugent of The Whitworth Art Gallery, Manchester, Liz Wilkinson at the V&A, Amy Meyers and Tim Goodhue at the Yale Center for British Art, Janice Slater at the National Gallery of Scotland, Katherine Williamson of Darlington Library. Finally, I would like to offer special thanks to Professor David Hill for reading drafts of the text.

The design of the catalogue and exhibition panels was carried out with his usual enthusiasm and innovation by Trevor Hatchett of Barron Hatchett Design, with photographs of objects from The Bowes Museum supplied by Syd Neville.

I would also like to acknowledge Durham County Council and the North East Regional Museums Hub who provide core funding for The Bowes Museum.

It is with enormous gratitude that I acknowledge the loan from the Yale Center for British Art, which enables this picture of Barnard Castle to travel to the place it depicts. This has been made possible with support from the County Durham Development Company and a number of private individuals.

Finally, a special thank you to the Friends of The Bowes Museum for their financial support both of the catalogue and the purchase with assistance from Virginia Surtees of *The History and Antiquities of the County Palatine of Durham* by Robert Surtees.

Adrian Jenkins

Director, The Bowes Museum

INTRODUCTION

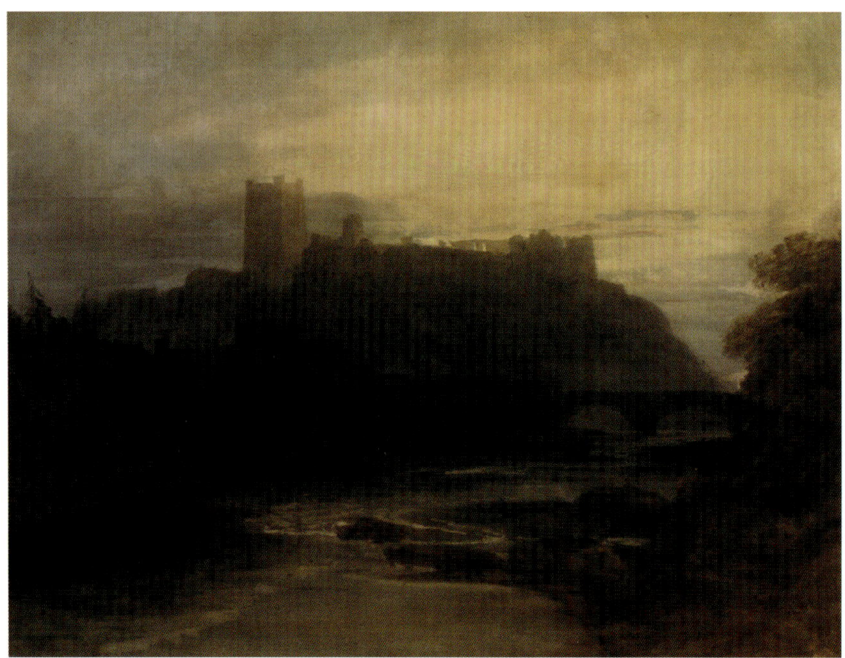

PLATE 1

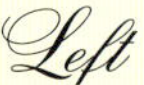

J. M. W. Turner

Richmond, Yorkshire, Sunrise: Colour Study

1799

Watercolour on paper

Tate, bequeathed by the artist 1856

TURNER USES A LOW VIEWPOINT IN *RICHMOND, YORKSHIRE, SUNRISE: COLOUR STUDY*, LOOKING ALONG THE RIVER TO THE TOWN ABOVE.

PLATE 2

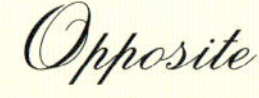

J. M. W. Turner

The Avenue, Farnley Hall

1815–1819

Watercolour, pencil, chalk, gouache and wash

Bolton Museum, Art Gallery & Aquarium

JOSEPH MALLORD WILLIAM TURNER (1775–1851) first toured the North of England in the summer of 1797, making sketches in Yorkshire, Durham and Northumberland, before visiting Harewood House where he was commissioned by Edward Lascelles to paint his country estate.[1] This first exploratory tour opened Turner's eyes to the region's varied and inspiring landscape and he continued to return to the North of England throughout his career. His interest in British landscapes was part of a contemporary rise in tourism within the home shores, itself the result of Britain's continuing wars with Napoleonic Europe which led to restrictions on travel abroad.[2] The North of England offered Turner some of his most lucrative commissions, allowing him to produce watercolours for engraved illustrations for a number of popular topographical books and antiquarian publications. The region became the source of some of Turner's most inspired and expressive landscape watercolours.

Following his initial trip, Turner continued to survey the North almost on an annual basis, returning to picturesque spots and examining locations from new viewpoints, as well as investigating further afield. Turner's early explorations led to a number of experimental watercolour studies developed from his sketches. In *Richmond, Yorkshire, Sunrise: Colour Study* (plate 1), Turner limits his palette to brown, grey and blue, silhouetting the well-known contours of Richmond Castle against the sky. The first rays of sunrise are subtly depicted, with horizontal washes in shades of red and blue.

History of the Original Parish of Whalley

Turner's first Northern commission for engravings came in 1799 when he was engaged to produce a number of images for the Reverend Thomas Dunham Whitaker (1759–1821) to illustrate the *History of the Original Parish of Whalley*, published in 1800 and 1801. The commission mentioned in Joseph Farington's (1747–1821) diary of 11 September 1799, which states that 'Turner now engaged by C. Towneley to go to Lancashire to make drawings of Whalley Abbey &c for a publication'.[3] His diary entry for 16 October 1799 suggests that Turner had completed a number of drawings for Whitaker of Whalley topics.[4] These images of antiquarian subjects must have been limiting in comparison to the colour studies and watercolours that Turner was making of Durham and Richmond. They do not give an indication of the wonderfully lavish landscapes that Turner was later to produce for Whitaker's *History of Richmondshire*. It would seem, at this time, that Turner was considered a junior draughtsman and the project was not without some difficulties. In a letter to Wilson of Clitheroe, Whitaker writes of a dispute between Charles Towneley and Turner. Mr. Towneley disliked the drawing that Turner had produced of the house at Gawthorpe and wished to replace it in the publication with what Whitaker describes as 'an old and very bad painting of Gawthorpe'.[5] Despite Whitaker's dislike for the image it was decided to put aside Turner's drawing for Towneley's choice.

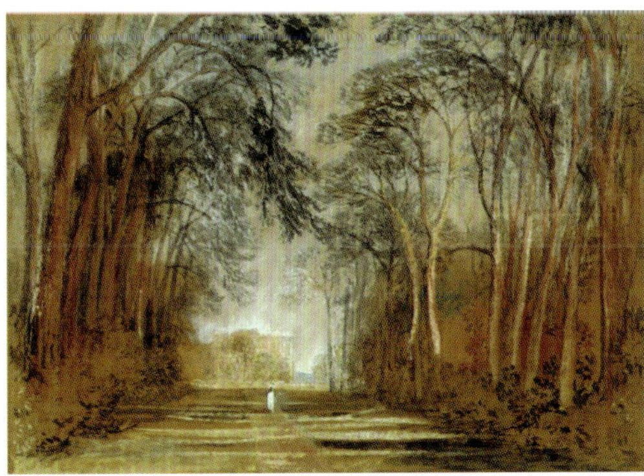

Farnley Hall

Although Whitaker's Whalley project may not have been professionally fulfilling for Turner, it did perhaps lead to one of the most important professional relationships of Turner's career. It is likely that Turner was introduced to Walter Fawkes (1769–1825) through one of his early patrons, Thomas Lister Parker of Browsholme Hall, for whom he had painted an image of the hall for Whitaker's *History of the Original Parish of Whalley*.[6]

In 1808 Turner was invited by Fawkes to stay at his country house, Farnley Hall, northwest of Leeds. Turner sketched Bolton Abbey on his way to Farnley and used the house as his base for sketching the surrounding area.

In 1808 following Turner's stay at Farnley, Fawkes commissioned twenty watercolours from Turner, ten of views of Yorkshire and ten of subjects from Turner's Alpine sketches, paying ten guineas for each image.[7] *Bolton Abbey, Yorkshire*, now in the University of Liverpool's art collection, is one of the ten Yorkshire views that Turner painted for Fawkes and is based on a large pencil study from 1808.[8]

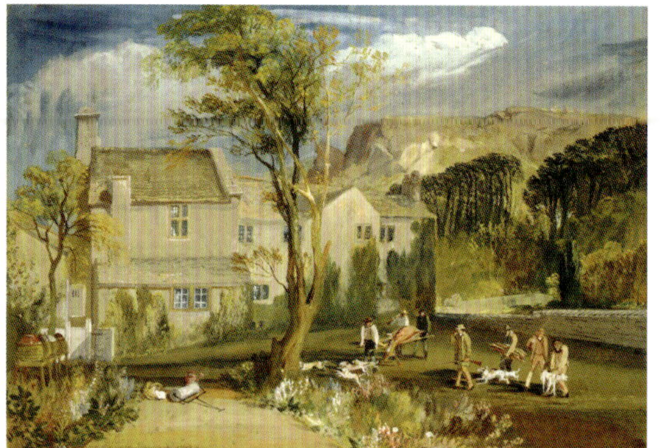

Turner stayed at Farnley almost every year from 1808 until Walter Fawkes's death in 1825. Their relationship grew from one of patron and artist into a strong friendship. Whilst staying with Fawkes Turner could relax from the pressures of London. He developed a great fondness for the Fawkes family and their estate, sketching the house and grounds on numerous occasions. *The Avenue, Farnley Hall* (plate 2) illustrates the eighteenth-century section of the house. Turner's use of a dark orange ground and densely layered sky give the impression of a crisp autumn day.

As Turner became more familiar with the Fawkes family and at home in their company, he began to take part in the leisurely pursuits of fishing and hunting and produced watercolours of daily life at Farnley. In his watercolour *Caley Hall, Yorkshire with Stag Hunters Returning Home* (plate 3) Turner illustrates huntsmen returning from a day's shooting with a large stag and boisterous dogs to Caley Hall, the Fawkes' hunting lodge. In the background Turner depicts more stags atop Caley Crags. Farnley was not only a base for some of Turner's sketching tours but would also furnish Turner's imagination with inspiration for some of his exhibition pieces. The crags and a thunderstorm that Turner witnessed whilst staying at Farnley are said to form the basis of *Snow Storm: Hannibal and his Army Crossing the Alps*, now in the collection of the Tate, London, which Turner exhibited at the Royal Academy in 1812.[9]

Fawkes engaged Turner to produce a watercolour to illustrate Sir Walter Scott's (1771–1832) poem *Rokeby* inspired by the Rokeby estate near Barnard Castle. Scott had first published *Rokeby* in 1813 increasing the popularity of Rokeby and the surrounding area where Turner had sketched on a number of occasions. In 1822 Turner worked on a number of sketches and colour studies, inscribing, not always accurately, the final watercolour (plate 4) with lines from the poem. Fawkes continued to purchase works from Turner until his death, commissioning a wide variety of subjects and encouraging Turner to work on an array of projects.

History of

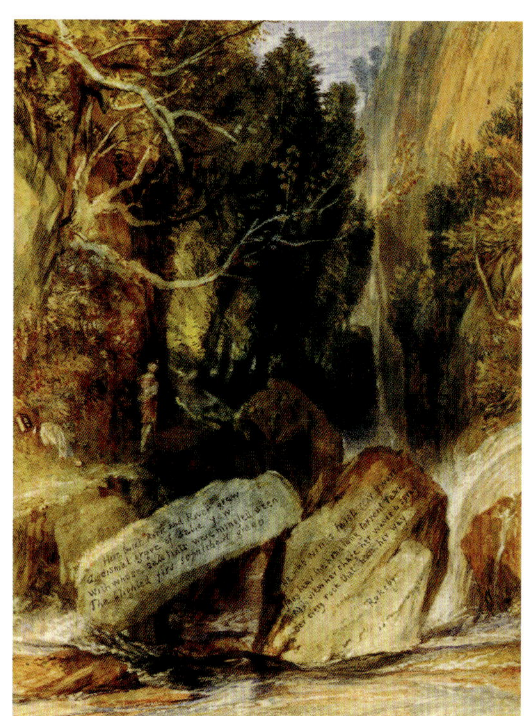

PLATE 3

Opposite, top

J. M. W. Turner

Caley Hall, Yorkshire with Stag Hunters Returning Home

circa 1818

Watercolour and gouache on paper

The National Gallery of Scotland

PLATE 4

Opposite, bottom

J. M. W Turner

Rokeby

1822

Watercolour on paper

Trustees of the Cecil Higgins Art Gallery, Bedford

Here, 'twixt Rock and River grew
A dismal grove of sable yew,
With whose sad tints were mingled seen
The blighted fir's sepulchral green,

He, who winds 'twixt rock and wave,
May hear the headlong torrent rave,
May view her chafe her waves to spray,
O'er every rock that bars her way.
Rokeby

Extract from *Rokeby* by Sir Walter Scott.

Richmondshire

In 1816 Turner received one of his most significant commissions when the publishers Longman & Co. engaged him to produce 120 views of Yorkshire for Whitaker's ambitious seven-volume *History of Yorkshire*, later reduced to the two-volume *An History of Richmondshire*. This continued their collaboration begun in 1799 with the *History of the Original Parish of Whalley*. However, by 1816 Turner was a widely admired artist. The inclusion of images engraved after his watercolours increased the desirability of Whitaker's publications and assisted in attracting essential pre-publication subscriptions. Turner negotiated extremely agreeable terms for his work, receiving twenty-five guineas for each watercolour.[10]

On 12 July of that year Turner left London, travelling northwards with a list of country estates and picturesque views that Whitaker and the publication's Committee had selected for him to sketch. He travelled by coach to Otley arriving at Farnley Hall the next day.[11] Turner kept a note of his travel expenses on the first page of his *Yorkshire 2* sketchbook paying 2s. 3d. for his breakfast in Doncaster.

After travelling for a few days in the company of the Fawkes family he parted company with them and began to visit the locations outlined in his commission for Whitaker's publication. It is difficult to judge how prescriptive the instructions Turner received were. He had sketched a number of the sites including Richmond and Easby on previous tours of the North. He judged it necessary to return to a number of locations to make new drawings. This may suggest that Turner was not only supplied with a list of locations but also guidelines detailing viewpoints. He had to work quickly over the summer months staying at each location for only one or two days, making preliminary sketches before moving onto the next spot. Turner required a large body of preparatory material in order to return to London and begin the required watercolours in his studio.

The project was extremely costly, and although initial subscriptions were promising, with all of the large copies being subscribed to, and takers for almost half of the 550 smaller copies,[12] after the publication of the first part in 1819 Longman & Co. reduced the print run of subsequent parts to between 71 and 77 for the large copies and to between 241 and 273 for the smaller copies.[13] Following Whitaker's ill health in 1820 and his continuing decline until his death in December 1821 the project seems to have been abandoned. Longman & Co. continued to publish sections until 1823 when the last part was issued with binding instructions, title page and indexes under the title *An History of Richmondshire*.

Picturesque Views in England and Wales

The disappointment that Turner felt after only twenty of his views of Yorkshire had been purchased and engraved for Whitaker's publication must have been severe. However, in 1825 Turner was engaged by Charles Heath to produce 120 images for engravings for *Picturesque Views in England and Wales*, a number of which were of northern subjects. He took the opportunity to work up sketches he had produced for Whitaker's project into watercolours for the engravings.

Turner based the watercolour *Barnard Castle* (plate 17) on drawings made in 1816. The image is bathed in daylight, silhouetting the castle and bridge in a sunlit haze against the sky. Turner has placed the viewer in an elevated position looking directly down the river, taking in its full breadth. The raised viewpoint is enhanced by the inclusion of a man to the right of the image, above two figures fishing. The man stands with one arm around the tree, supporting himself, the other outstretched holding a knife ready to cut back the branches of the tree.

In another image for the England and Wales series *Brinkburn Priory, Northumberland* (plate 5) Turner has again included figures fishing as an illustrative device to bring his composition to life. The

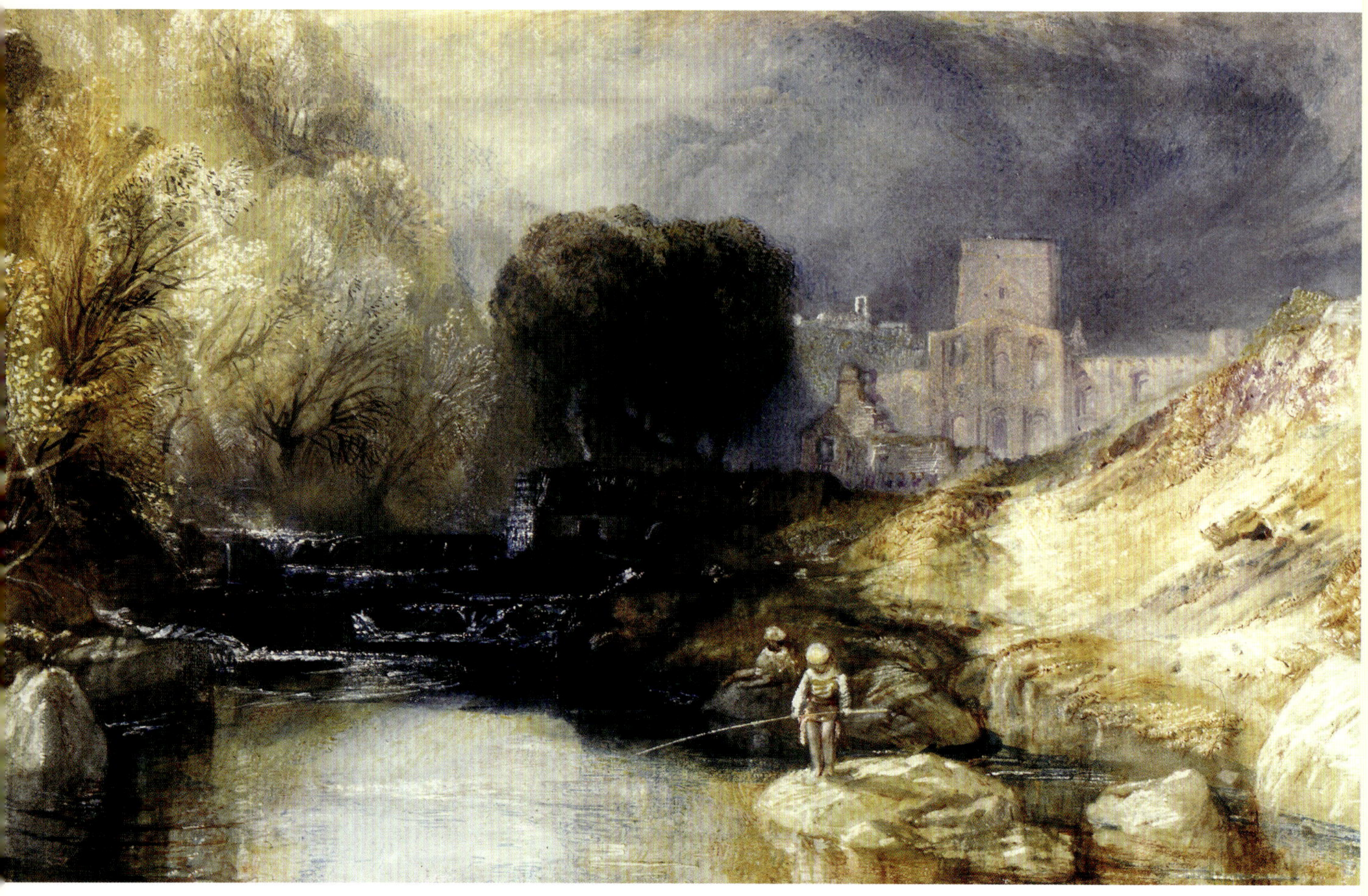

PLATE 5

Left

J. M. W. Turner

Brinkburn Priory, Northumberland

circa 1830

Watercolour on paper

Sheffield Galleries & Museums Trust

PLATE 6

Opposite

Samuel Rawle

(1771 – 1860)

Raby Castle

Engraving after J. M. W. Turner

The Bowes Museum

inclusion of pictorial devices such as these often represent ideas of a rural idyll and do not reflect the demanding daily tasks that many people living in the countryside faced.

Picturesque Views of England and Wales encountered a number of financial difficulties. The publisher Hurst and Robinson went bankrupt in 1826 and the project was sold to Moon, Boys and Graves before being taken over by Longman & Co. In 1838 after ninety-six plates had been issued in twenty-four parts, the project was finally abandoned by Longman & Co.[14] Turner purchased all of the remaining stock of prints and plates when they were put up for auction in 1839. During the printing process the quality of the engraving plate deteriorated. In an attempt to protect his reputation and avoid inferior prints entering the marketplace, Turner destroyed a large number of engraving plates.

The History of Durham

In 1817 Turner received a commission from Lord Darlington for an oil painting of Raby Castle. Whilst making preparatory sketches for the oil painting, Turner was asked to produce a watercolour image of Raby for inclusion as an engraving in Robert Surtees's (1779–1834) *The History and Antiquities of the County Palatine of Durham*. As part of this publication three further images, one of Hylton Castle and two versions of Gibside, were commissioned by John Bowes, the 10th Earl of Strathmore, to illustrate his Durham country properties.[15]

In a letter postmarked 21 November 1817 to James Holworthy, Turner wrote of events in late October, commenting 'Lord Strathmore called at Raby and took me away to the north'.[16] Whilst staying with the Earl of Strathmore at Gibside, Turner sketched the property from vantage points from the south and north. His sketchbook [CLVI] on this tour had elongated pages providing him with broad sheets that were perfect for sketching panoramic landscapes. Turner worked across both sheets outlining sweeping views across Gibside. His studies detail the sloping hills that extend across the landscape, creating a scenic backdrop for Gibside House.

In his text to *The History and Antiquities of the County Palatine of Durham* Surtees noted that:

> *It is not easy to convey any adequate idea of the magnificent woodland scenery of Gibside. Woods, venerable in their growth and magnificent in their extent, sweep from the heights of the hills to the brink of the Derwent, intersected by the deep irregular ravines.*[17]

In Turner the Earl of Strathmore had engaged an artist who could rise to the challenge of rendering the splendour of the natural landscape on paper. Turner produced a watercolour drawing from each vantage point, offering the Earl the opportunity to choose which image to include in Surtees's book. In both the watercolour drawing from the south (plate 7) and the north (plate 37) Turner punctuates the natural landscape with a number of architectural features.

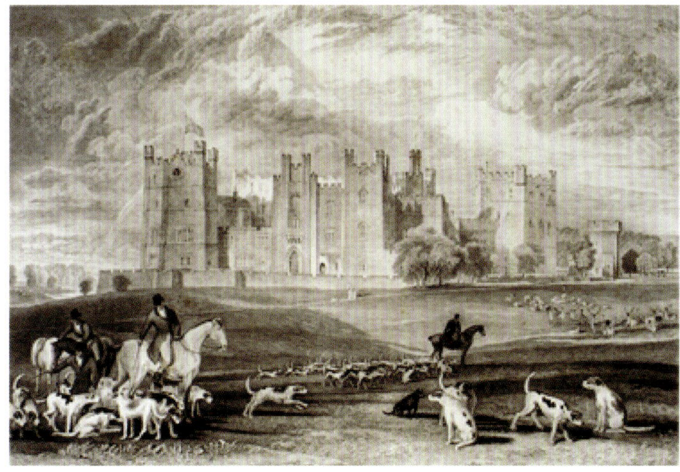

Surtees's description printed alongside Turner's image gracefully acts as praise for Turner's impression of Gibside as well as admiring and honouring the Bowes family's enhancement of the landscape. Surtees noted 'the few artificial objects introduced are sufficiently grand and distinct not to disgrace the noble scenery which surrounds them'.[18] Turner paid special attention to these architectural additions, making small detailed studies of the Column of Liberty and Gibside Chapel on a page in his sketchbook.

In the watercolour *Gibside from the North* Turner expertly depicts the Derwent River to the right of the picture, drawing the viewer's eye into the image. To the left Turner includes a young boy to draw the viewer towards one of the focal points (plate 8). The boy crouches, leaning over the bank where the water tumbles down into the ravine below. A stone wall, across the water from the boy, supports the riverbank and alludes to the river's ability to erode and reshape the landscape. Turner builds up the image's perspective with a carefully controlled palette. In the background Turner renders the woods and fields in subtle shades of green, yellow and blue accentuating the lushness of the land. He introduces stronger shades as he builds up the middle ground and uses deep browns and reds in the foreground to depict the exposed earth of the valley's side.

From the two watercolours produced by Turner, the Earl of Strathmore selected *Gibside, County Durham, the Seat of the Earl of Strathmore* drawn from the southwest of the property, to illustrate Surtees's publication. The scene is framed by trees above a gentle incline on the left of the watercolour. In contrast to the undulating landscape in *Gibside from the North*, this view gracefully outlines the land as it sweeps across the image. Following excavations at Pompeii and Herculaneum in the mid-eighteenth century and the publication of a number of finely illustrated volumes, society developed a taste for classically inspired architecture. The inclusion of the woman in classical robes carrying a Grecian vase in the foreground and the neo-classically designed Gibside Chapel above, mirrors the elegance of the landscape and echoes a contemporary interest in Antiquity.

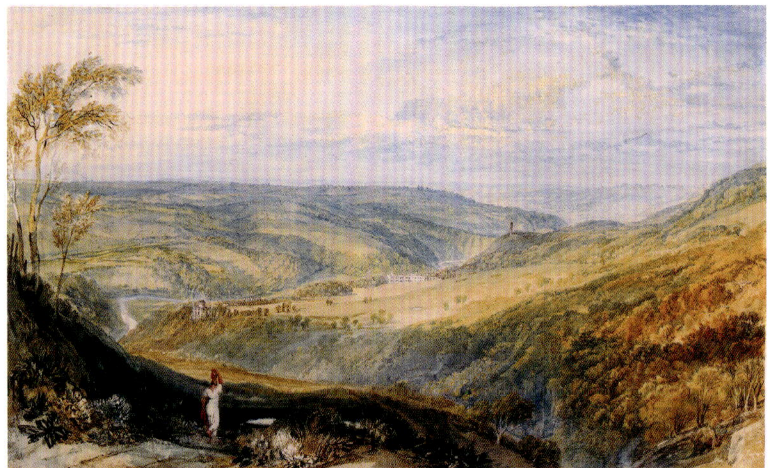

PLATE 7

Opposite

J. M. W. Turner

Gibside, County Durham, The Seat of The Earl of Strathmore

circa 1817

Watercolour on paper

The Bowes Museum

PLATE 8

Right

Detail

J. M. W. Turner

Gibside from the North

circa 1817

Watercolour on paper

The Bowes Museum

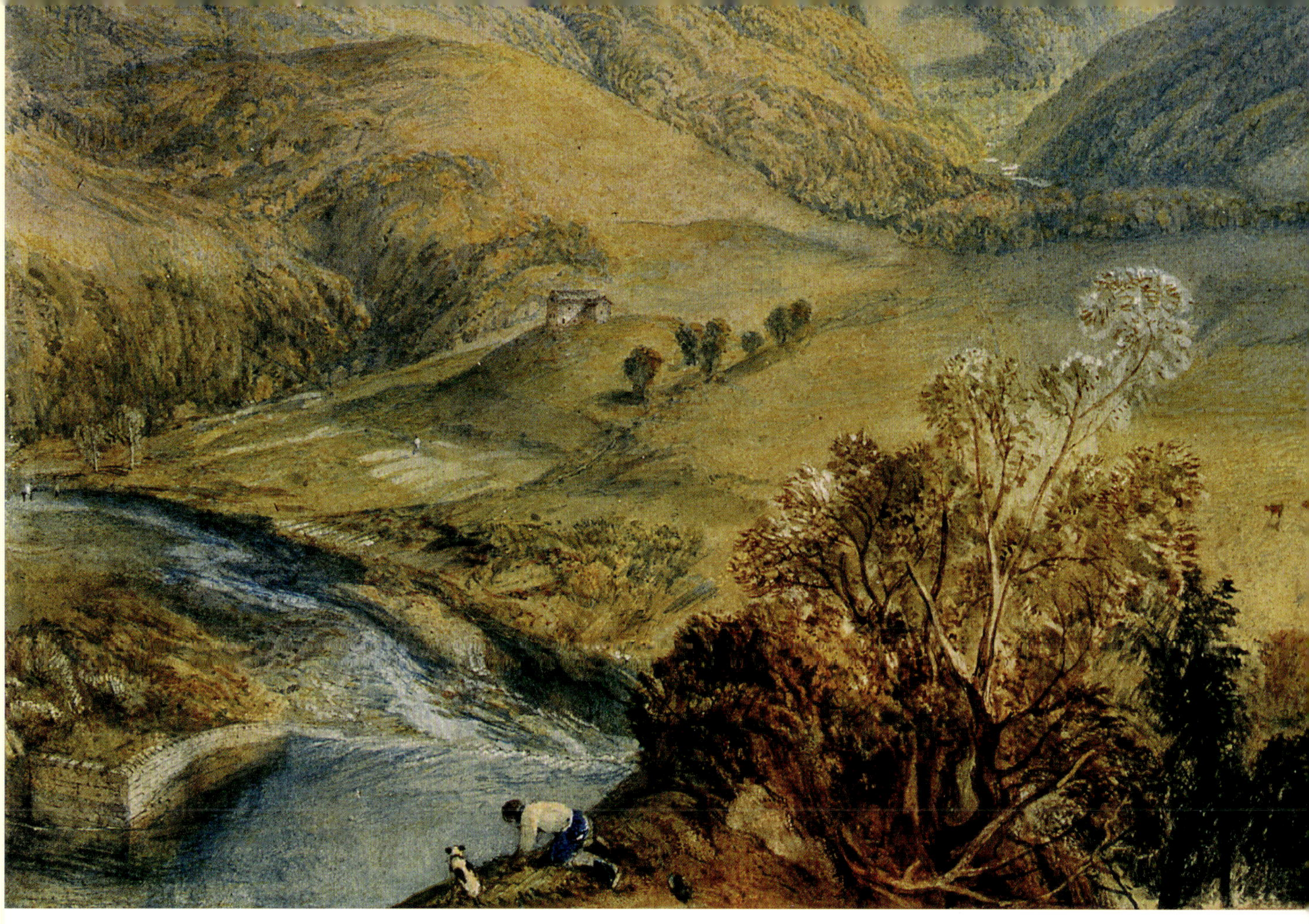

Turner often worked on a wide variety of projects concurrently, preparing watercolours and proofing engravings for publication, fulfilling private commissions and producing oil paintings for annual exhibition and display at his London gallery. Turner's numerous watercolours for engraving projects were produced solely for publication. The watercolours were rarely exhibited and were only known to the public in their printed form. However, his watercolours of Northern subjects are some of his most striking and memorable landscapes. Through their publication as engravings many of the beauty spots of the North captured by Turner are made available to society. They have continued to inspire travellers and artists to journey to the North of England.

Retracing Turner's Sketching Tours

A Topographical Journey

by Michael Rudd

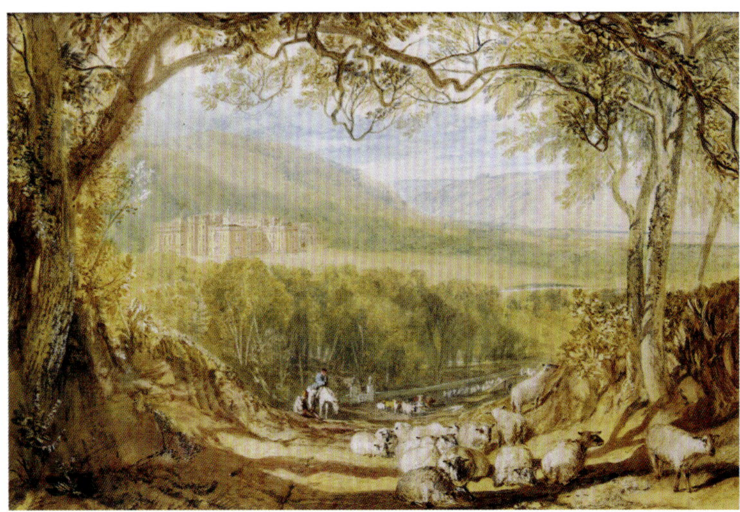

PLATE 9

Left

J. M. W. Turner

Aske Hall

circa 1816

Watercolour on paper

Private collection

PLATE 10

Opposite

J. M. W. Turner

Gibside from the South

Pencil on paper

Raby sketchbook, Tate, bequeathed by the artist 1856

WHEN WORKING IN HIS STUDIO, TURNER'S VISUAL MEMORY WAS QUITE REMARKABLE: SOMETIMES DETAILS ONLY HINTED AT IN A SKETCH FIND THEIR FULL EXPRESSION IN THE CORRESPONDING WATERCOLOUR.

IN CONSIDERING J. M. W. TURNER'S TOPOGRAPHICAL WATERCOLOURS, it is instructive, if not essential, to examine carefully the corresponding sketches, and compare these with the actual landscape. Although the subjects for the Whitaker's Richmondshire and Surtees's Durham commissions were chosen for the artist, even here Turner explored each location and chose his viewpoints for detailed sketches. It is interesting to speculate that Turner, in leaving his sketchbooks to the nation as part of his will, perhaps intended that his whole creative process from sketch to finished watercolour or engraving should be available for examination.

When visiting the locations with copies of the relevant sketches in hand, Turner's craftsmanship is soon apparent. The artist, while faithfully indicating the topography – walls, hedges, trees and buildings – often seamlessly merges into one sketch these details from more than one viewpoint. The foreground details may often be found either hundreds of metres away,[1] or in another sketchbook.[2] The main compositional sketches often spill over on to a facing page to take in a wide panorama. While Turner often jots down notes regarding colours, or records items such as 'loose rocks' or 'corn', there is usually little indication of the weather; occasionally figures are included. Details of buildings and sometimes animals are found alongside the main sketches; whole pages are sometimes filled with such details.

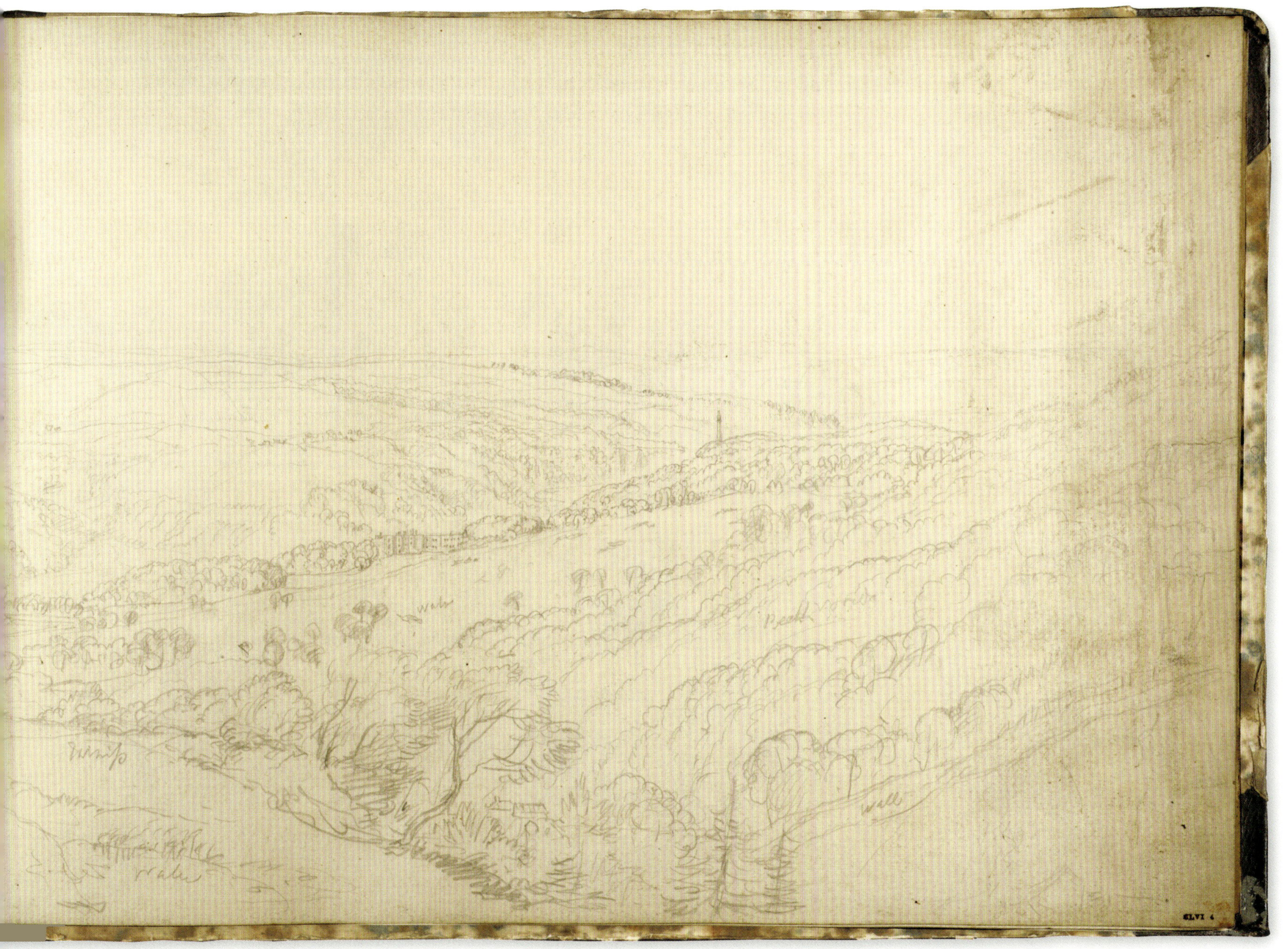

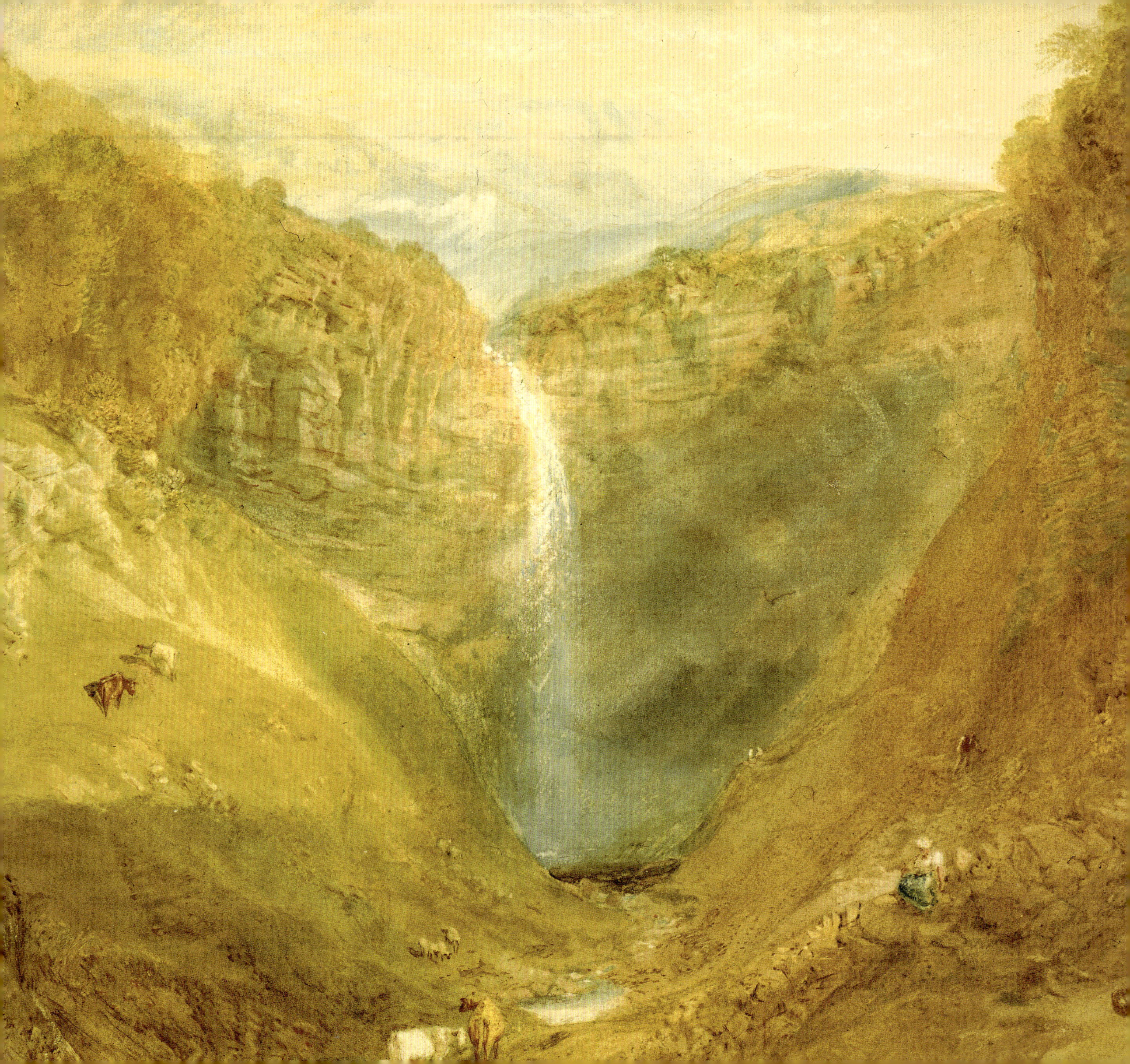

PLATE 11

Right

J. M. W. Turner

St Agatha's Abbey near Richmond, Yorkshire

circa 1817

Watercolour over graphite with some scraping-out on buff-toned paper

The British Museum

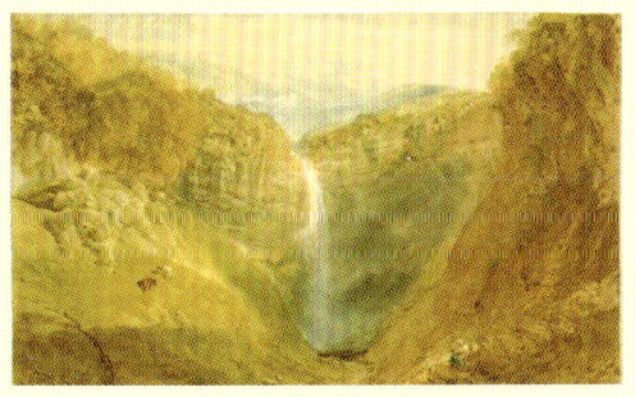

PLATE 12

Opposite

Detail

J. M. W. Turner

Hardraw Fall

circa 1816 – 1818

Watercolour on paper

The Syndics of the Fitzwilliam Museum, Cambridge

IT IS INTERESTING TO SPECULATE THAT TURNER, IN LEAVING HIS SKETCHBOOKS TO THE NATION AS PART OF HIS WILL, PERHAPS INTENDED THAT HIS WHOLE CREATIVE PROCESS FROM SKETCH TO FINISHED WATERCOLOUR OR ENGRAVING SHOULD BE AVAILABLE FOR EXAMINATION.

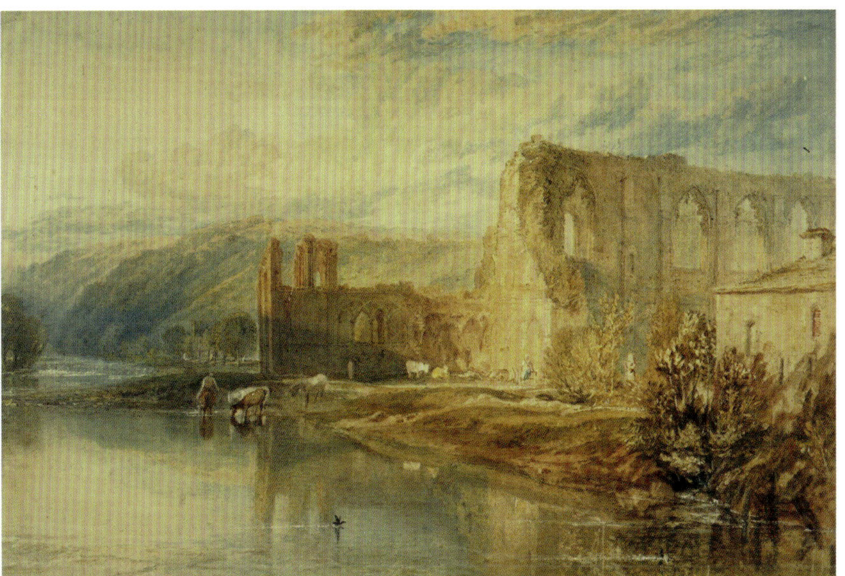

When working on his watercolours in the studio, Turner not only combined elements from sketches made many years apart,[3] but also from those made many miles apart.[4] The artist's visual memory was quite remarkable; sometimes details only hinted at in a sketch – a chimney, a wall – find their full expression in the corresponding watercolour.[5]

In connection with the works in this exhibition, Turner used the following sketchbooks[6] which formed part of bis bequest to the nation in 1856:

1797	**North of England**	[XXXIV]	270 x 230 mm
	Tweed and Lakes	[XXXV]	370 x 274 mm
1816	**Yorkshire 2**	[CXLV]	154 x 96 mm
	Yorkshire 4	[CXLVII]	122 x 203 mm
	Yorkshire 5	[CXLVIII]	173 x 260 mm
1817	**Raby**	[CLVI]	232 x 328 mm
	Durham, North shore	[CLVII]	116 x 188 mm
	Itinerary Rhine Tour	[CLIX]	56 x 106 mm
1830	**Rokeby and Appleby**	[CCLXIV]	75 x 94 mm

This discussion arranges Turner's sketches chronologically, offering the opportunity to analyse each location separately, over a number of years. Through historic discussions, present-day visits and contemporary photographs, we explore Turner's sketches and resulting watercolours and engravings.

1797

North *of* England

TURNER'S TOUR IN THE SUMMER OF 1797 took him to Yorkshire, County Durham, Northumberland and the Lake District. The sketchbooks are full of architectural or topographic details, with no evidence of the artist exaggerating vertical scale. These are studies largely for exhibition watercolours.

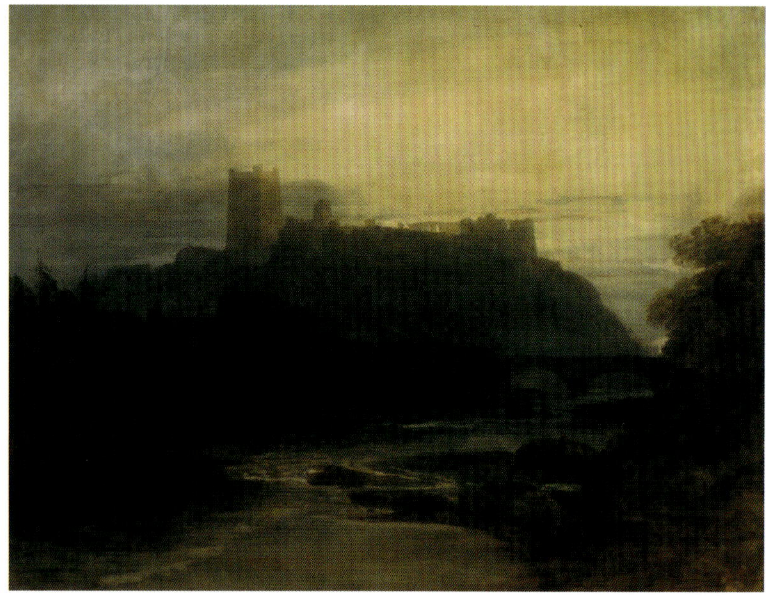

Richmond

LABELLED 'RICHMOND Y' BY TURNER, the sketch [XXXV 9] from the banks of the River Swale is a detailed study of the castle above the bridge. The details are simplified in the watercolour (plate 13). Despite trees obscuring the view, we can still find Turner's viewpoint today, upstream from the Green or Richmond Bridge.

PLATE 13

Left

J. M. W. Turner

Richmond, Yorkshire, Sunrise: Colour Study

1799

Watercolour on paper

Tate, bequeathed by the artist 1856

PLATE 14

Opposite

W. R. Smith

Richmond, Yorkshire

1819

Engraving after J. M. W. Turner

The Bowes Museum

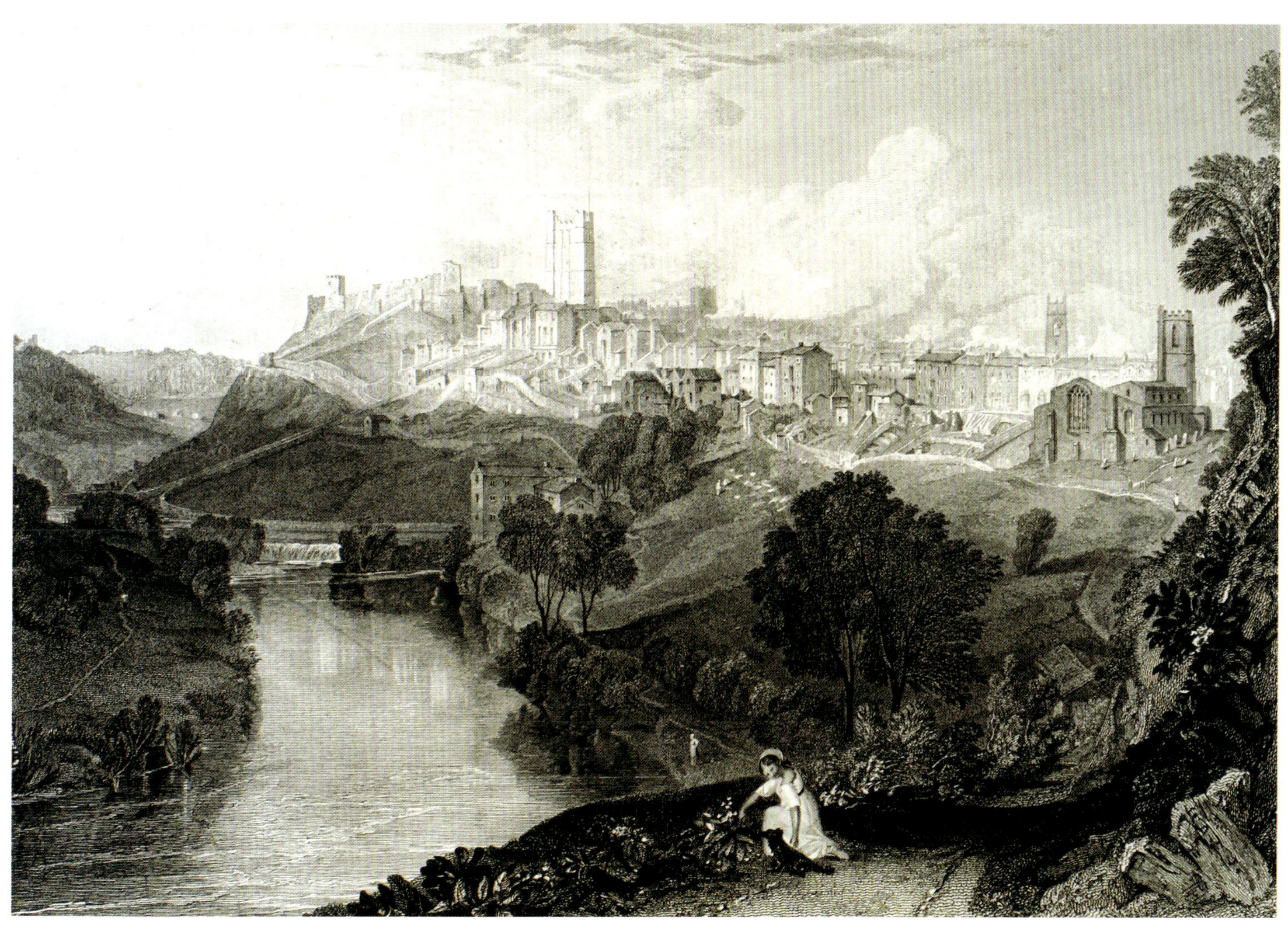

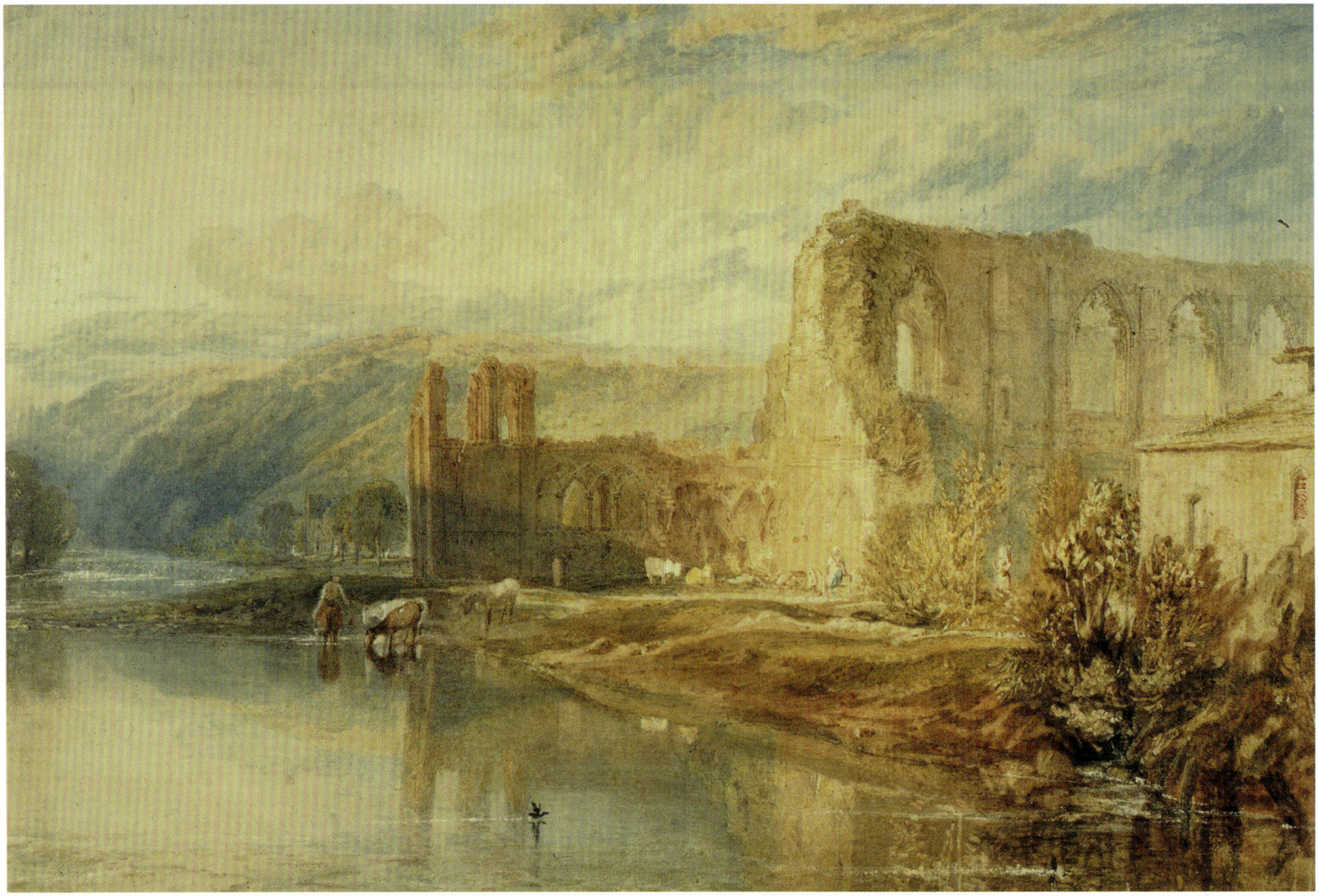

St Agatha'a Abbey, Easby

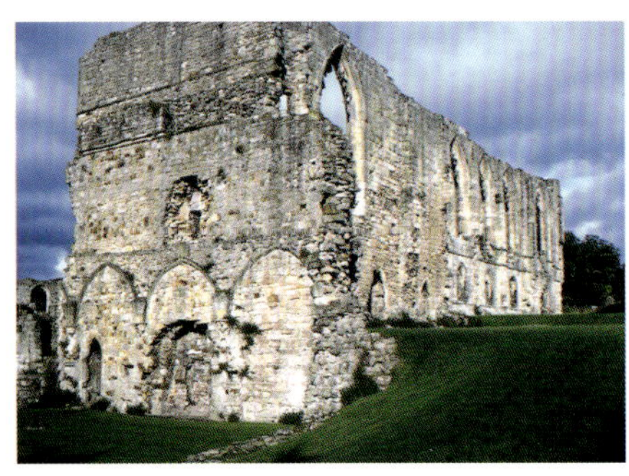

Of the three sketches Turner made at St. Agatha's Abbey near Richmond, one was worked up into a watercolour, perhaps on the spot, another was the basis of an exhibition watercolour, while the third [XXXIV 25] was not used until the artist produced the watercolour for his Richmondshire commission (plate 15). Although trees obscure much of the scene from Turner's viewpoint, the details of his sketch can be found by exploring the site. We can still see the cracked and leaning wall of the west range and the magnificent windows of the refectory; the building on the right of the sketch and watercolour was apparently once the monks' granary.[7]

PLATE 15

Opposite, top

J. M. W. Turner

St Agatha's Abbey near Richmond, Yorkshire

circa 1817

Watercolour over graphite with some scraping-out on buff-toned paper

The British Museum

PLATE 16

Opposite, bottom

Easby Abbey

Contemporary photograph

Michael Rudd

PLATE 17

Right, top

J. M. W. Turner

Barnard Castle

circa 1825

Watercolour on paper

Yale Center for British Art, Paul Mellon Center

PLATE 18

Right, bottom

Barnard Castle

Contemporary photograph

Michael Rudd

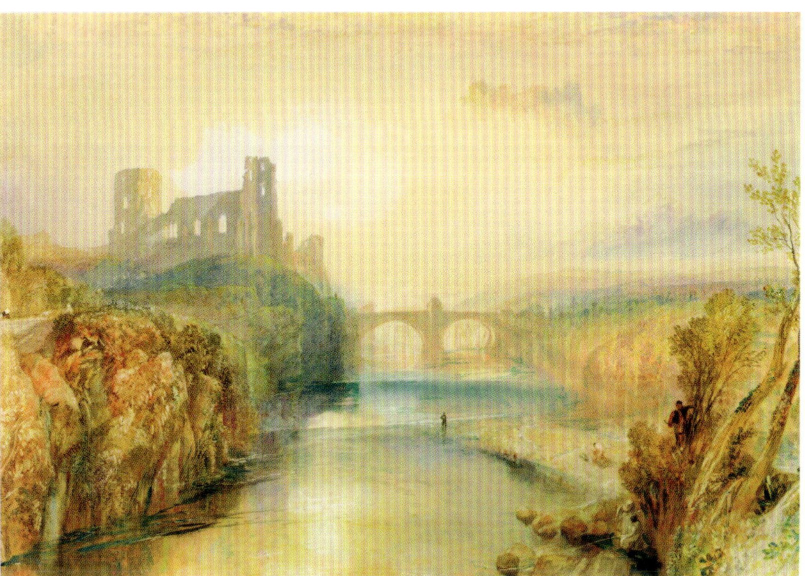

Barnard Castle

TURNER MADE TWO DETAILED STUDIES of the castle above the bridge in his *North of England* sketchbook. Both sketches show a building, perhaps a chapel, on the bridge [XXXIV 29] from upstream and [30] from downstream. This building is missing from the sketch made in 1830 in the *Rokeby and Appleby* sketchbook [CCLXIV 55a] (plate 38), but is used in the watercolour of around 1825 (plate 17). For the sketch upstream of the castle, access to the river is rather difficult, the aqueduct or 'Water' bridge affords a viewpoint similar to, although higher than, Turner's. The view from downstream is from near Thorngate Bridge.

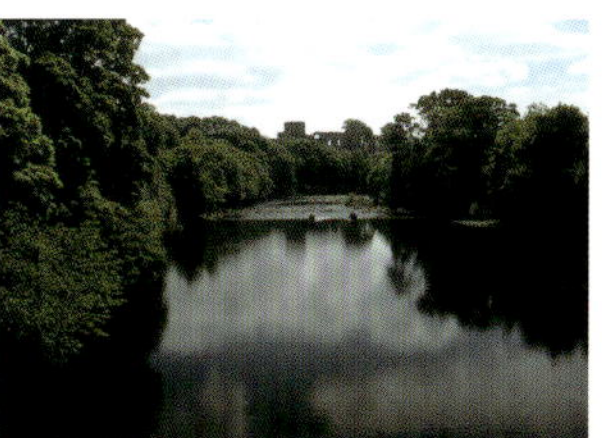

Durham Cathedral

TURNER MADE EIGHT SKETCHES in the City of Durham. The watercolour *Durham Cathedral from the river*, now in the collection of the Royal Acadamy of Arts, is based directly on the sketch [XXXV 15] with its carefully observed details of the Cathedral, Castle and the buildings at the end of Framwellgate Bridge.

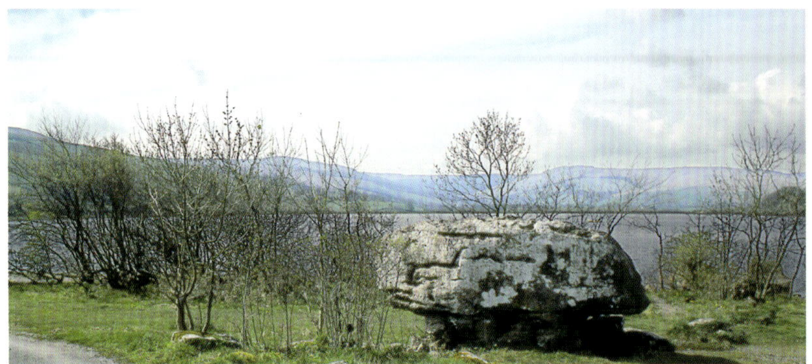

1816

Richmondshire

In 1891 the engraved copper plates of Richmondshire were reworked and published by H. Virtue & Company as *Richmondshire Illustrated by Twenty Line Engravings after Drawings by J.M.W. Turner, R.A. with Descriptions by Mrs. Alfred Hunt.* Mrs. Hunt's father, Dr. Raine of Crook Hall, Durham was one of the committee that chose the subjects for the Richmondshire project. As Mrs. Hunt compared the engravings with the scenes sketched only 75 years previously, her comments can sometimes be useful; we have a further 115 years of changes in the landscape with which to contend.

In comparison with the sketches of 1797, those of 1816 show more exaggeration of vertical scale; slopes are steeper than in reality and the height of towers is increased.

Mrs. Hunt gives an interesting commentary on the way in which landscape was viewed in the eighteenth and early nineteenth centuries. At the time, 'it was almost the whole duty of all hill scenery to inspire alarm, and every painter or writer who wished to give a good impression of any particular place always painted it, or wrote of it, as if it were twice its real size.' [8]

This 'impression' was achieved by exaggerating hill slopes, by compressing the width of a scene, or diminishing the size of animals or people to dramatise nature. However, when comparing Turner's sketches with the scene today, or with the finished watercolours, we must also remember that these watercolours were prepared for purposes of engraving to a certain size to fit the relevant book; compression of the width of a scene was inevitable.

It is in the sketchbooks used on this tour of 1816 that we find Turner exploring his subjects from a number of viewpoints. By including his viewpoints in a series of sketches, Turner was able to visually re-construct his exploration of a site. This tour started when he left the Fawkes party at Malham on 25 July 1816.[9]

PLATE 19

Left

Semer Water

Contemporary photograph

Michael Rudd

PLATE 20

Opposite

J. M. W. Turner

Simmer Lake, near Askrigg

circa 1817

Watercolour with some scraping-out on paper

The British Museum

26 July 1816

Simmer Lake

Coming over the Stake Pass from Wharfedale, Turner took out his small pocket-book to make a quick sketch[10] of Thwaite End House with its dilapidated roof looking over Semer Water to two farms along Marsett Lane. There are two other sketches in the pocket-book, one so rough it may even have been done while the artist was still on his horse.[11] Turner used his medium-sized *Yorkshire 4* sketchbook for his main sketch of the lake, with the Carlow Stone in the foreground, and labelled 'Simmer Water' [CXLVII 3]. The lake is quite full, almost to the Carlow Stone, but today debris indicates that the lake level can rise even higher than this, and the summer of 1816 was very wet. In the sketch Turner includes the Stake Road with the two barns which he had passed, as well as the buildings he had sketched earlier. There are no Devil's finger marks on the Carlow Stone,[12] no hints of the weather conditions, and none of the wealth of figures and cattle that he later adds to his watercolour (plate 20).

Leaving the lake foreshore Turner dismounted to sketch from the road to Askrigg;[13] on a second detailed sketch in *Yorkshire 4*[14] he shows his route down Stake Road, over Semer Water Bridge and through Countersett. Later that day, at the King's Head in Askrigg, he may have learned of the two legends of Semer Water[15] and recalled these when painting the watercolour.

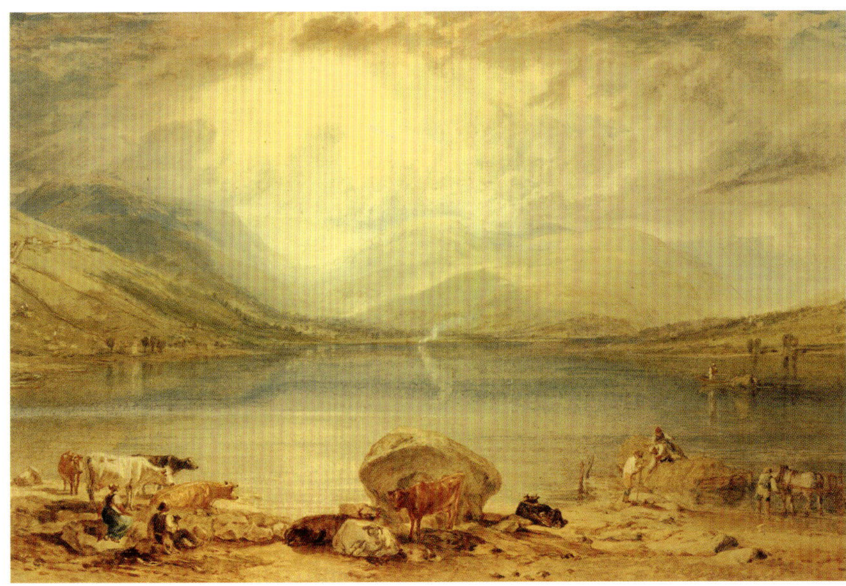

28 July 1816

Hardraw Fall

THE WATERCOLOUR (PLATE 21) IS BASED ON A WIDE VIEW stretching over two pages of the large *Yorkshire 5* sketchbook[16] as the artist tries to capture the scale of this waterfall. Turner relies on a closer sketch in the same book for details of the rock strata and the pulsing waves of the falling water [CXLVIII 15]. From these viewpoints in the gorge leading from the Green Dragon Inn up to the waterfall it is impossible to see the hillside Turner sketches in above the lip of the fall. This skyline, more carefully depicted in CXLVIII 28a, is of the limestone scars on Abbotside Common further to the north east and visible from nearer the inn at which Turner was staying.

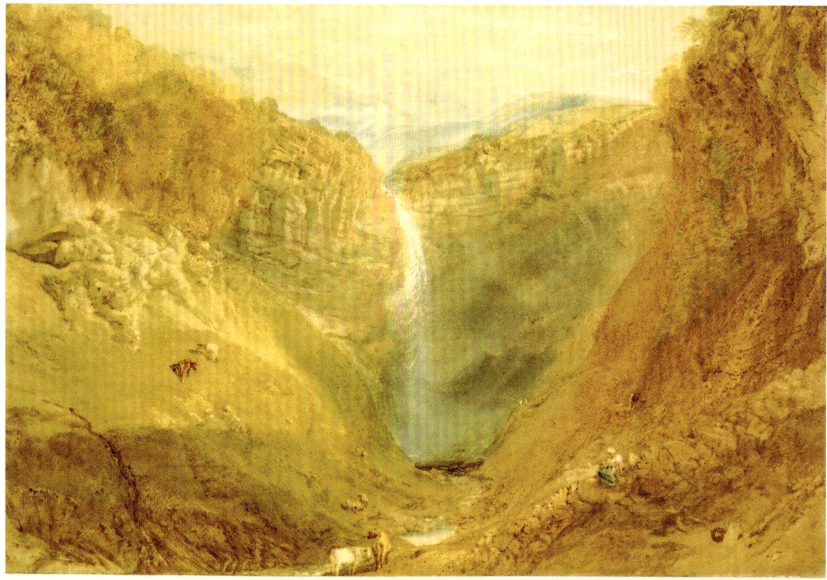

29 *to* 31 July 1816

Richmond

TURNER STOPPED BRIEFLY ON HIS WAY FROM WENSLEYDALE to Richmond to make a quick sketch of the distant town from the west. Approaching the town he made another two sketches in his small pocket-book of the castle and bridge, having made a large sketch here in 1797, before riding up Cornforth Hill to the Kings Head. As the main town in Richmondshire, Longman & Co. seem to have required four views of the town as well as one of Easby Abbey.

PLATE 21

Opposite

J. M. W. Turner

Hardraw Fall

circa 1816 – 1818

Watercolour on paper

The Syndics of the Fitzwilliam Museum, Cambridge

PLATE 22

Right

J. M. W. Turner

St. Agatha's Abbey, Easby, Yorkshire: colour study

circa 1820

Watercolour on paper

Tate, bequeathed by the artist 1856

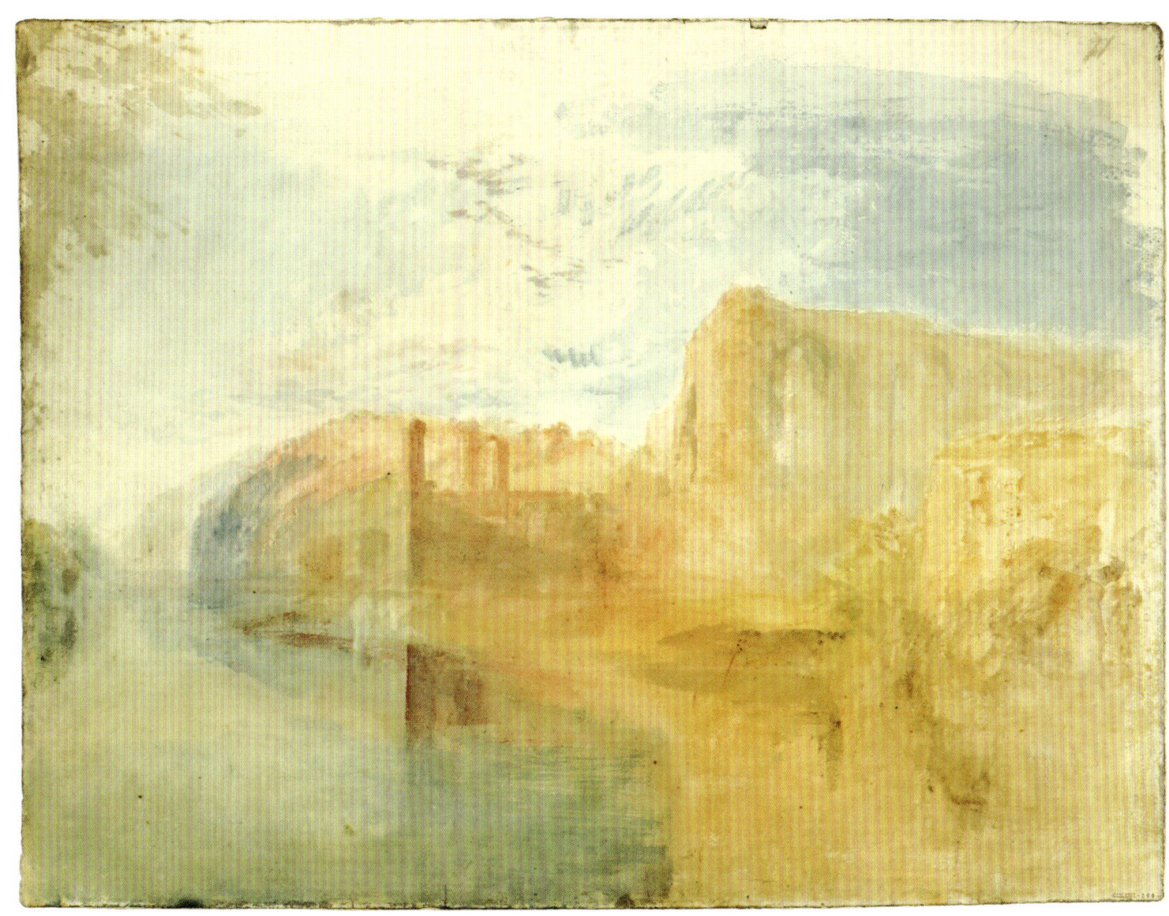

St. Agatha's Abbey, Easby

THAT EVENING, USING ALL THREE SKETCHBOOKS, Turner made eight drawings of the Abbey at Easby, exploring different viewpoints. For the watercolour (plate 15), however, the artist returned to a sketch made on his 1797 tour,[17] along with one from his pocket-book of the same scene [CXLV 112], where a bend in the river gives a large expanse of water in the foreground. This sketch includes the belfry of the small parish church of St. Agatha's, but Turner does not include this in the watercolour.

Aske Hall

THE BASIS FOR THE WATERCOLOUR (PLATE 23) IS A SKETCH in the *Yorkshire 4* sketchbook [CXLVII 23]. Despite the growth of trees, Turner's viewpoint along the road from Richmond to Gilling West is identifiable today. The buildings among trees on the far left, the skyline and the general topography are confirming pointers.

For the park gates and the foreground framing trees, still easily identifiable today where the road is bounded by higher banks, Turner refers to his smaller *Yorkshire 2* pocket-book [CXLV 110a]. A comparison with the watercolour shows that Turner retains the twisted branches arching over the road, as well as details of the tree trunks. The next page [CXLV 111] includes a detailed study of the Hall, along with sketches of Aske Bridge and the lake with rotunda – all essential elements of the watercolour. A single line is sufficient to remind the artist of the wall that retains the lawn in front of the Hall. Turner makes no use of the three double-page studies in his *Yorkshire 3* sketchbook.

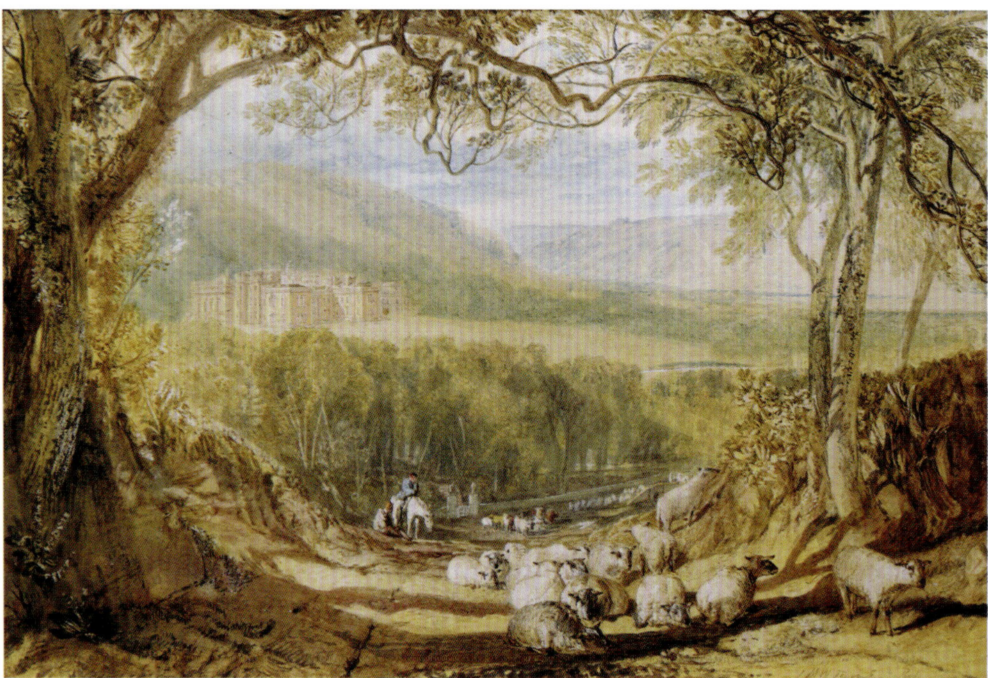

PLATE 23

Left

J. M. W. Turner

Aske Hall

circa 1816

Watercolour on paper

Private collection

THE PARK GATES AND THE TREES OF ASKE HALL ARE STILL EASILY IDENTIFIABLE TODAY WHERE THE ROAD IS BOUNDED BY HIGHER BANKS. A COMPARISON WITH THE WATERCOLOUR SHOWS THAT TURNER RETAINS THE TWISTED BRANCHES ARCHING OVER THE ROAD, AS WELL AS DETAILS OF THE TREE TRUNKS.

PLATE 24

Opposite

J. M. W. Turner

Richmond, Yorkshire

circa 1816

Watercolour on paper

Victoria & Albert Museum

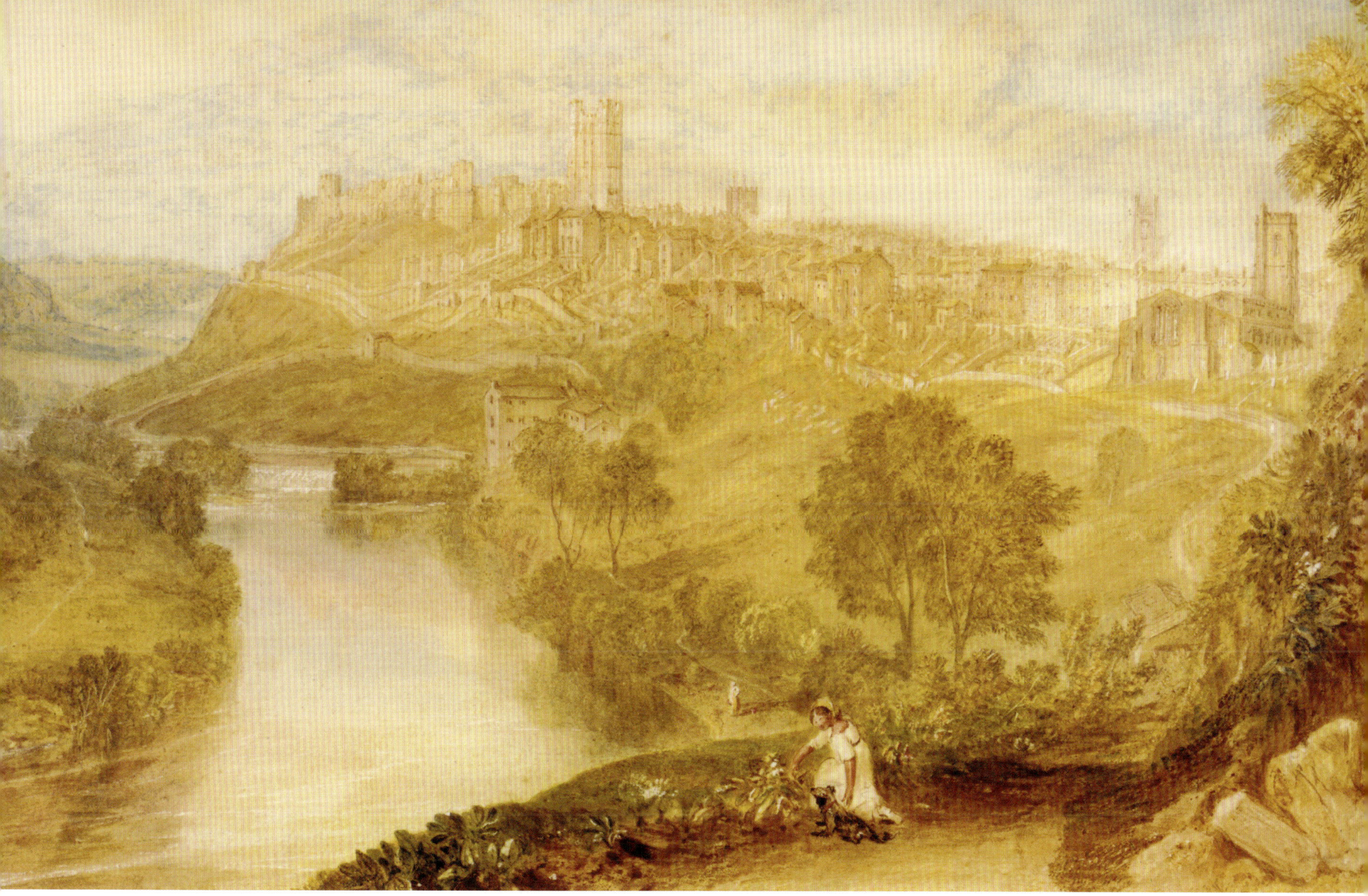

Richmond, Yorkshire

FOR HIS FOURTH STUDY OF RICHMOND Turner used his largest sketchbook [CXLVIII 10a – 11]. Although trees have grown, St. Mary's church was heavily restored in 1858, Mercury Bridge was not built until 1836 and the mill is no longer, enough remains for us to identify Turner's viewpoints. Leaving St. Mary's he traces the path past a cottage to 'Loose Rock' at the side of the track towards Easby. Characteristically, the artist includes the three viewpoints he had used the previous day for studies of the town – from near Boggy Lane, from the south east looking over the cascade, and from past Hudswell to the west.

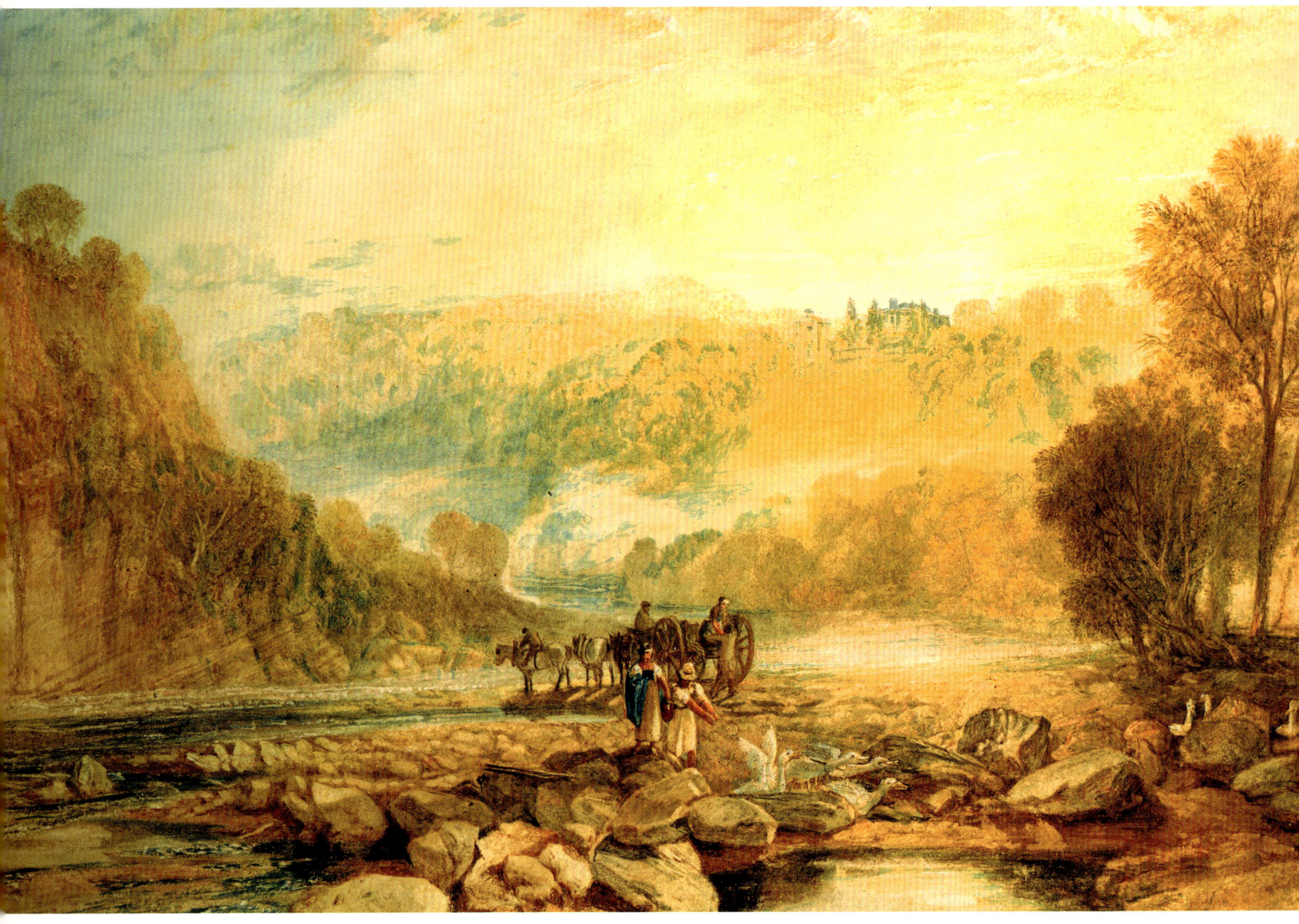

PLATE 25

Opposite

J. M. W. Turner

Wycliffe, near Rokeby

circa 1816

Watercolour

Walker Art Gallery, National Museums Liverpool

PLATE 26

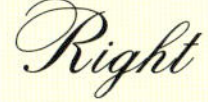

John Pye

(1782 – 1874)

Junction of the Greta and the Tees at Rokeby

1819

Engraving after J. M. W. Turner

The Bowes Museum

WORKING IN THE RAIN, TURNER MADE FIVE QUICK SKETCHES OF THE BANKS OF THE GRETA AT ROKEBY AND OF MORTHAM TOWER. MRS. HUNT CORRECTLY IDENTIFIED TURNER'S VIEWPOINT WHICH IS NOW ON PRIVATE LAND. NOW ONLY THE STUMPS REMAIN OF THE THREE LARGE ELMS WHICH GUARD THE HOUSE.

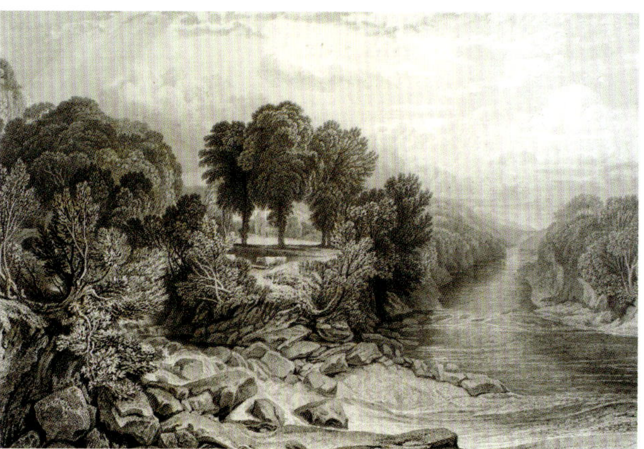

JUNCTION *OF THE* GRETA *AND THE* TEES *AT* *Rokeby*

AT ROKEBY NEAR GRETA BRIDGE the very wet conditions in the summer of 1816 seem to have limited Turner's usually meticulous sketching. Working in the rain, Turner made five quick sketches of the banks of the Greta at Rokeby[18] and of Mortham Tower,[19] and only one sketch in his large sketchbook [CXLVIII 29a]. Even here, there are only a few quick notes of the channels of the rocky Greta and the Tees, with the trees suggested; Turner's apparent failure to sketch Rokeby itself or the Prospect House at Dairy Bridge over the Greta can be seen in the watercolour and the engraving (plate 26).

Mrs. Hunt correctly identified Turner's viewpoint 'by the many-channelled Greta, on the Mortham side' although today this is on private land. By 1891 'the three large elms which guard the house had grown considerably since Turner's time';[20] now only their stumps remain.

1 AUGUST 1816 *Wycliffe, near Rokeby*

WHEN PRODUCING THE COMMISSIONED WATERCOLOUR OF WYCLIFFE (plate 25), Turner used his first sketch [CXLVII 26] of 'Wycliffe' above the wooded sides of the 'calm' river Tees, building on the few 'Ston[es]' sketched and noted. On a continuation of this sketch on the next page [27] in the sketchbook, Turner records two people on horses and a cart passing cottages on the lane. In the watercolour, he retains one of the cottages but moves the cart to a prominent position, along with the geese and girls no doubt remembered from that day.

Today access to Turner's viewpoint is on private land, but the churchyard affords a view of Wycliffe Hall similar to that in Turner's sketch. The river still washes directly beneath the cottage with its two chimneys and extension (and its 1779 date stone), and the lane leading to the river ford is still recognisable. For details of 'Wycliffe House' Turner used another page [29] in his sketchbook, where he sketches the Hall on the same page as a study of Brignall church, his next objective.

Brignall Church

FROM GRETA BRIDGE WE CAN FOLLOW in the artist's footsteps as he walked upstream beside and then above the River Greta towards the small church of Brignall. It was to be rebuilt eighteen years later nearer the hamlet of Brignall, leaving only ruins and the churchyard behind. Despite the inevitable growth of trees we can identify the spot where Turner recorded his first sight of the secluded church beside the river below with Brignall Banks beyond. It was the sketch [CXLVII 29a] labelled 'Bignall' that was subsequently used for the main composition of the watercolour and engraving (plate 27). One of the two nearer views furnished details of the church and the trees next to the river,[21] although for the churchyard wall and gravestones, still there today, Turner relied on his memory, for there is no indication of these in any of the sketches.

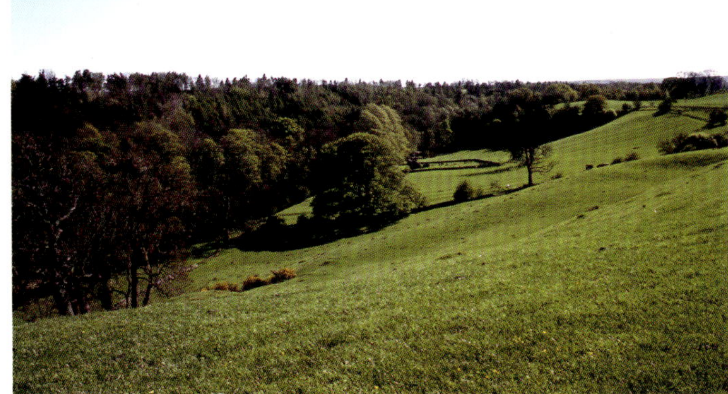

PLATE 27

Opposite

Samuel Rawle

(1771 – 1860)

Brignall Church

1821

Engraving
after J. M. W. Turner

The Bowes Museum

PLATE 28

Opposite

Brignall

Contemporary photograph

Michael Rudd

DESPITE THE INEVITABLE GROWTH OF TREES WE CAN IDENTIFY THE SPOT WHERE TURNER RECORDED HIS FIRST SIGHT OF THE SECLUDED CHURCH BESIDE THE RIVER BELOW WITH BRIGNALL BANKS BEYOND. IT WAS THIS SKETCH THAT WAS SUBSEQUENTLY USED FOR THE MAIN COMPOSITION OF THE WATERCOLOUR AND ENGRAVING.

2 AUGUST 1816

Barnard Castle

THE COMPOSITION OF THE WATERCOLOUR (plate 17) dating from around 1825 is based on a sketch in the *Yorkshire 4* sketchbook [CXLVII 32], showing the castle and bridge from upstream. However, it seems as if Turner also relied on two sketches in the small pocket-book [CXLV 103 & 103a], as well as sketches made on his tour of 1797,[22] when he recorded the building in the middle of the bridge.

From Barnard Castle, the sketches show that Turner went on to Bowes before making for Middleton-in-Teesdale, Low Force, High Force and Cauldron Snout.

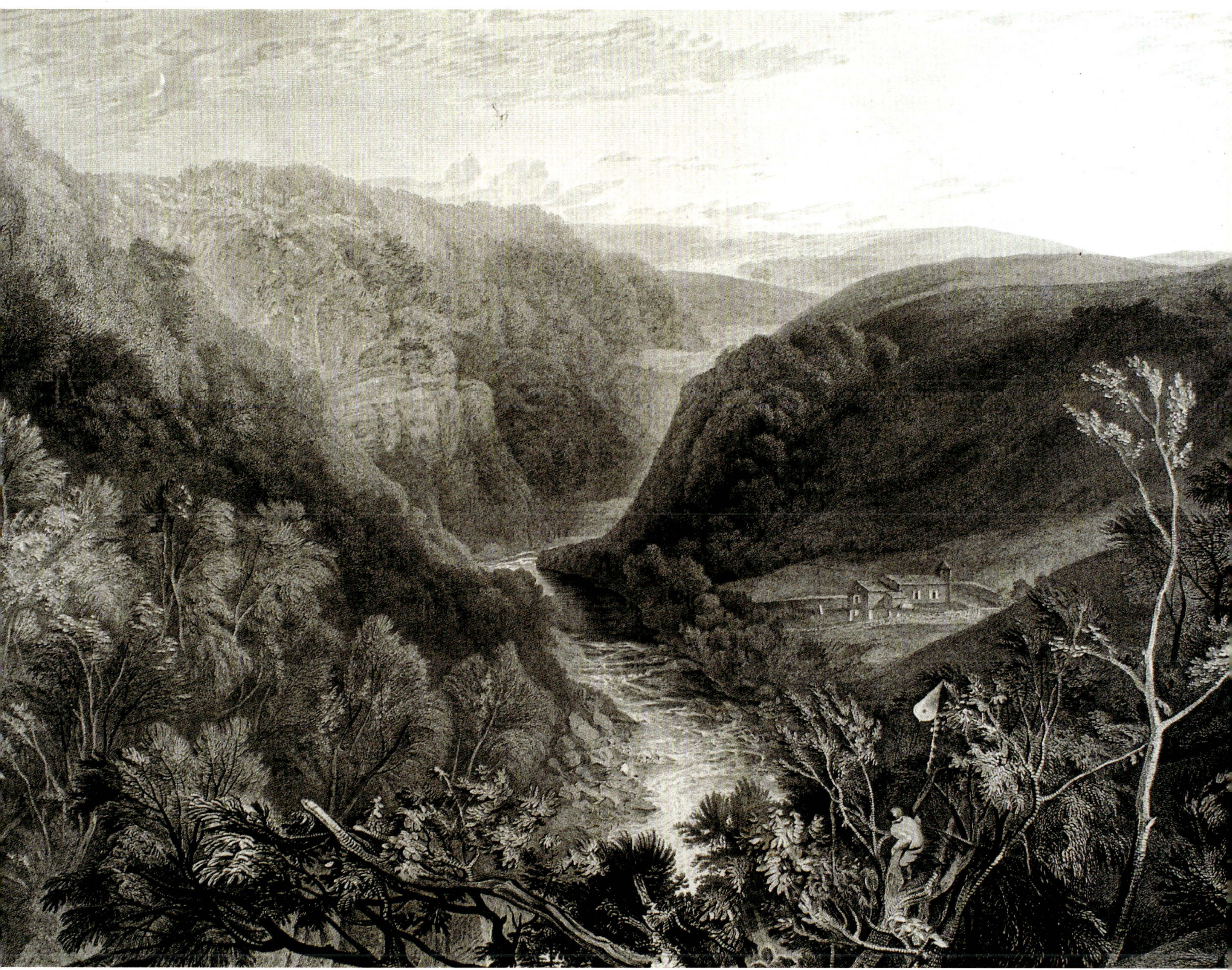

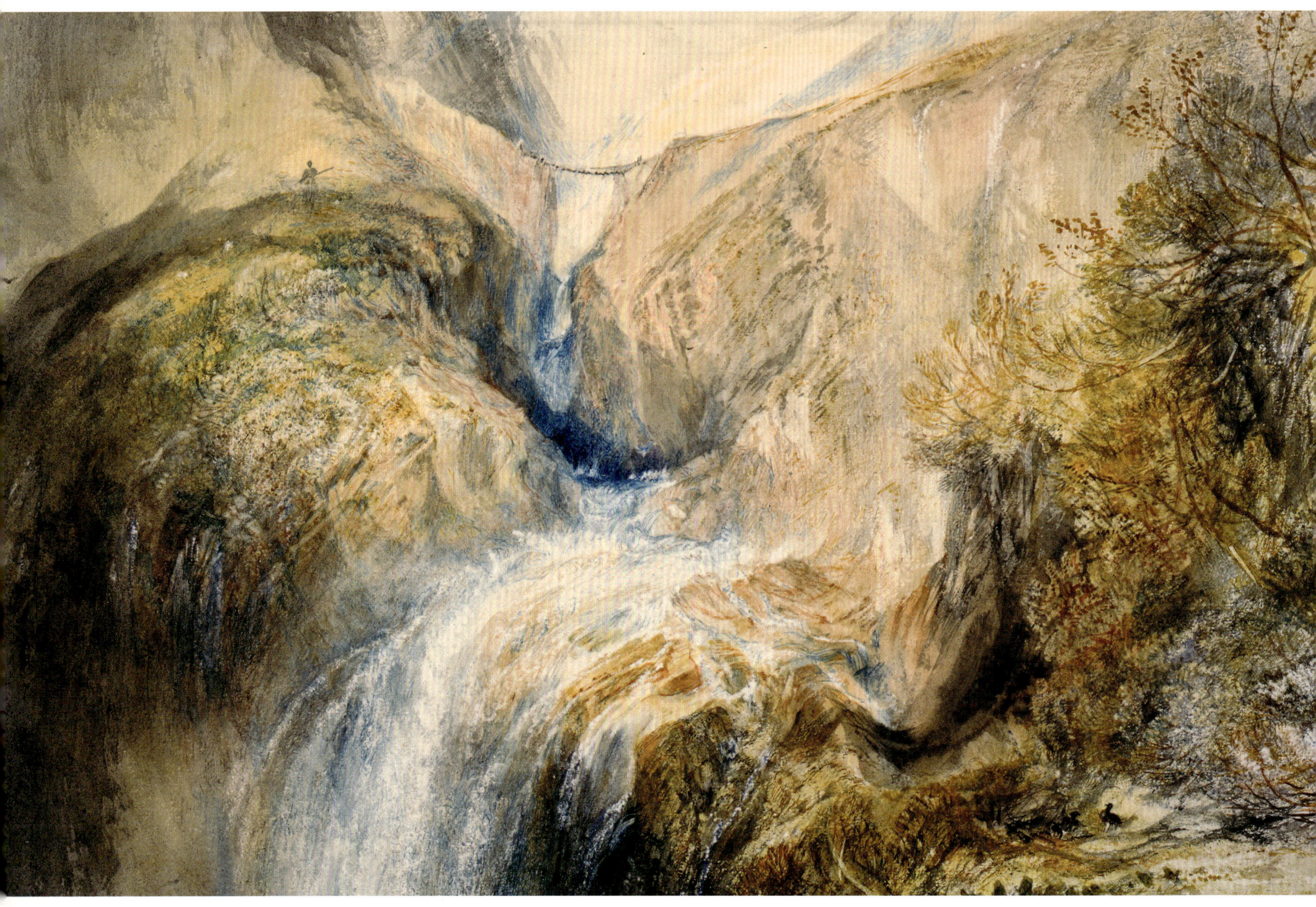

PLATE 29

Opposite

J. M. W. Turner

Chain bridge over the Tees

circa 1836

Watercolour on paper

The Whitworth Art Gallery, The University of Manchester

Right

Wynch Bridge

Contemporary photograph

Michael Rudd

3 August 1816

Chain Bridge over the River Tees

WHEN IN 1836 TURNER CAME TO PAINT A WATERCOLOUR OF Cauldron Snout he used his sketch made twenty years previously in his *Yorkshire 5* sketchbook [CXLVIII 6a]. Here the artist has sketched the staircase of falls over the columnar Whin Sill from a number of viewpoints and combined them into one; he shows the planked bridge – a 'sublime' viewpoint for tourists at the time.

In the watercolour (plate 29) there is no evidence of the columnar rocks, nor of the pool at the foot of the falls; the planked bridge is replaced with a chain bridge of the title. Here Turner recalled the eighteenth century Wynch Bridge that he had sketched [CXLV 102] earlier the same day; its shape fitted more easily into his transformed composition. This small rain-marked, economical sketch faithfully shows Low Force, the hills beyond and the chains of the bridge; Turner's note '20' perhaps refers to the number of vertical supports. Trees obscure Turner's precise viewpoints today and the bridge was rebuilt in 1830 slightly upstream and at a higher level.[23]

From upper Teesdale Turner had to negotiate bleak moors and later the crossing of the sands of Morecambe Bay to Hest Bank before reaching Lancaster.

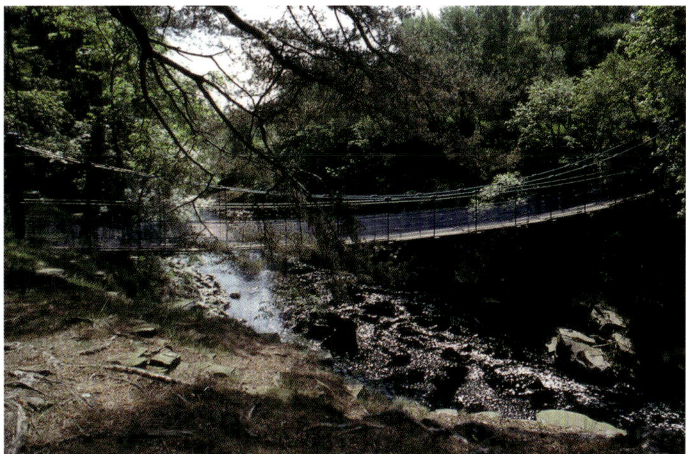

8 August 1816

Heysham and Cumberland Mountains

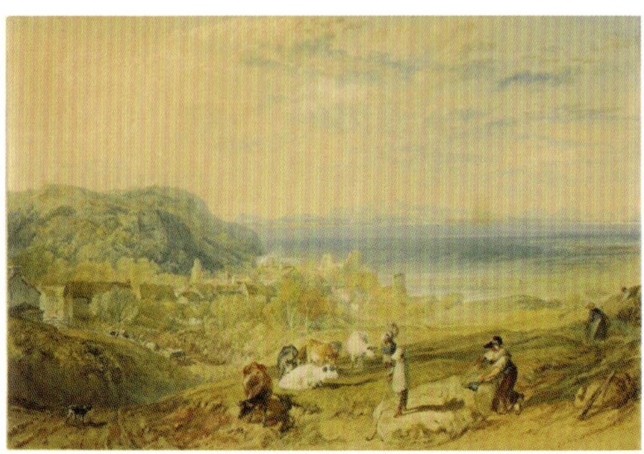

At Heysham, Turner, in his small pocket-book, first explored the foreshore[24] with its 'Red Scar', 'Sand', 'Black rocks', and looking up to the ruins of St. Patrick's Chapel (dating from the eighth to tenth centuries) and St. Peter's Church with its belfry. While exploring the farm buildings of the village,[25] built of the sandstone and gritstone quarried locally, some then thatched with ling, and some today displaying their seventeenth century date stones, Turner appears to have seen a possible viewpoint from which he could see the village, the headland behind and also across Morecambe Bay to the Lake District fells.

From this slightly higher ground towards the east of the village, and working on two pages in the *Yorkshire 4* sketchbook [CXLVII 40a – 41], Turner was able to review his journey of the previous few days, apparently consulting a map to note 'Black Combe', Coniston 'Old Man', 'Holker' Hall, 'Floo'kburgh, 'Castle H'ead and 'Arnside' on a panoramic sketch which has to be extended above the main sketch. Perhaps the commissioned watercolour (plate 30) was to include this panorama, as it receives attention from Whitaker, 'a diversified horizon, nearly two hundred miles in circuit, and extending from Llandudno... to the summit of Helvellyn, with all the intermediate outlines of pointed fells, jutting promontories, and retiring bays.'[26] Here we can see Turner's manipulation of the scene. In the sketch, as well as altering the position of the panorama of fells in relation to Heysham, he compresses it, then in the watercolour moves it further and omits the extension with Arnside.

Heysham has developed so much since 1816 that it is difficult to find the exact viewpoints that Turner uses to sketch the farms along Main Street leading down to the foreshore, along with the headland and St. Patrick's Chapel. Certainly the position along Knowlys Road known as 'Turner's View' is a likely spot for one of the viewpoints, leading down as it does towards Main Street. Here Turner notes the lane complete with hay wain and gate which are used in the watercolour. This location, with grassland today, is perhaps where Turner remembered cows grazing on the poorest land along the edge of the coast and which he introduced into the watercolour.

As Turner had made a fairly detailed record of St. Peter's Church in the view of Heysham in his pocket-book[27] only the belfry receives much attention here. A full study of the church was engraved for Whitaker's Richmondshire; similarly engraved were the rock-cut graves near St. Patrick's Chapel, not visible from Turner's viewpoints.[28]

PLATE 30

Left

J. M. W. Turner

Heysham and Cumberland Mountains

1818

Watercolour,
with some scraping-out
on paper

The British Museum

PLATE 31

Opposite

W. R. Smith

Heysham and Cumberland Mountains

1822

Engraving
after J. M. W. Turner

The Bowes Museum

From upper Teesdale, Turner had to negotiate bleak moors and later the crossing of the sands of Morecambe Bay to Hest Bank before reaching Lancaster.

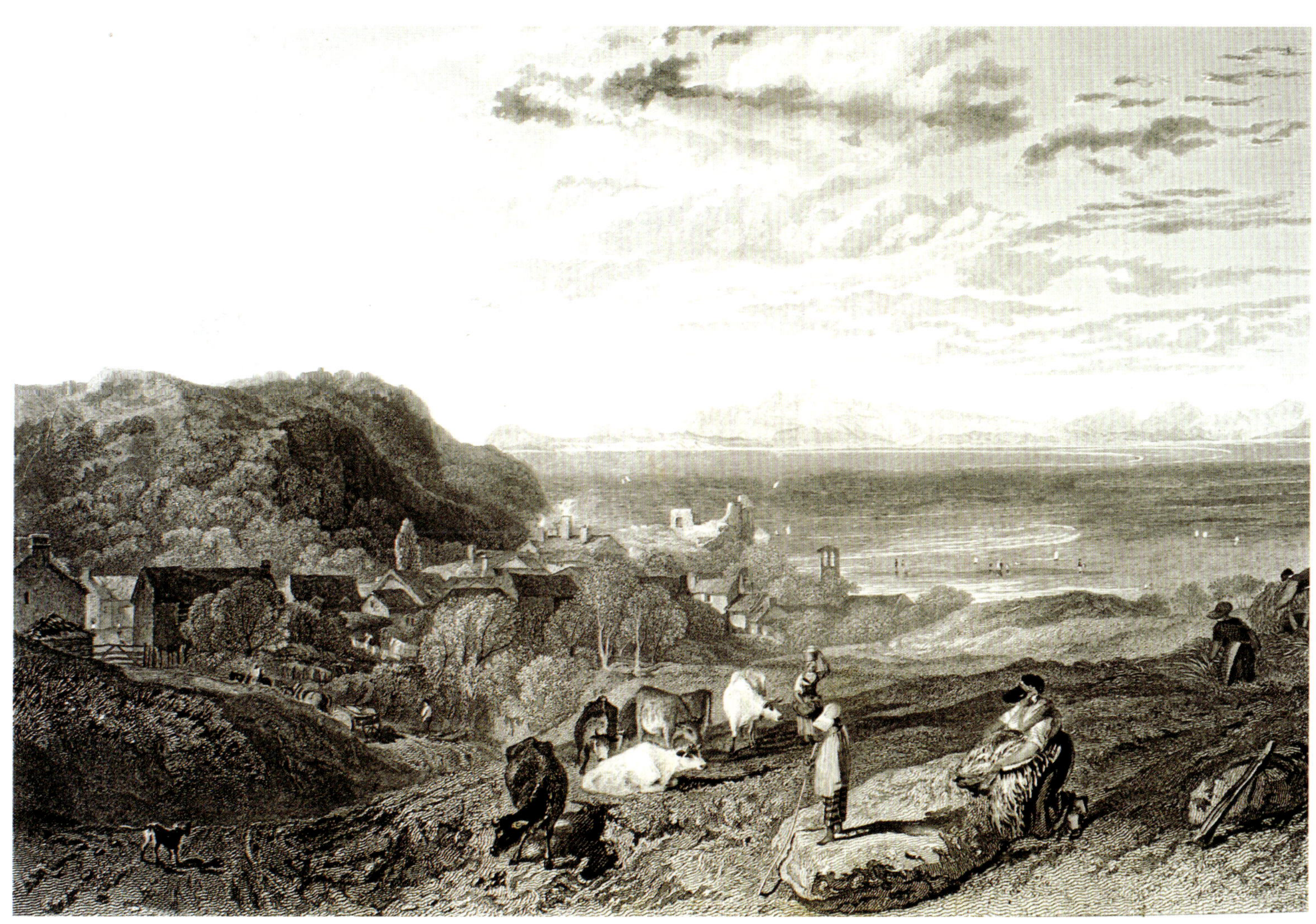

9 August 1816

Hornby Castle from Tatham Church

From Lancaster Turner had two commissioned views to make along the Lune valley. At first he made a preliminary sketch of Hornby from near the bridge at Tatham. Today from the now five-arched bridge we can see the 'stones' the artist noted forming a weir in the River Wenning, with Low Tatham Church beyond the meadows of the flood plain, and Hornby Castle peeping above the tall trees planted on its eastern side. Of Tatham Whitaker wrote, 'The situation of the church, the hall, and the parsonage, is delightful; as there is, perhaps, no point from which Hornby Castle is seen to greater advantage.'[29] It was perhaps from the bridge here that Turner decided he required a better viewpoint than the church would provide; he would have been able to see the inn further up the road. Trees

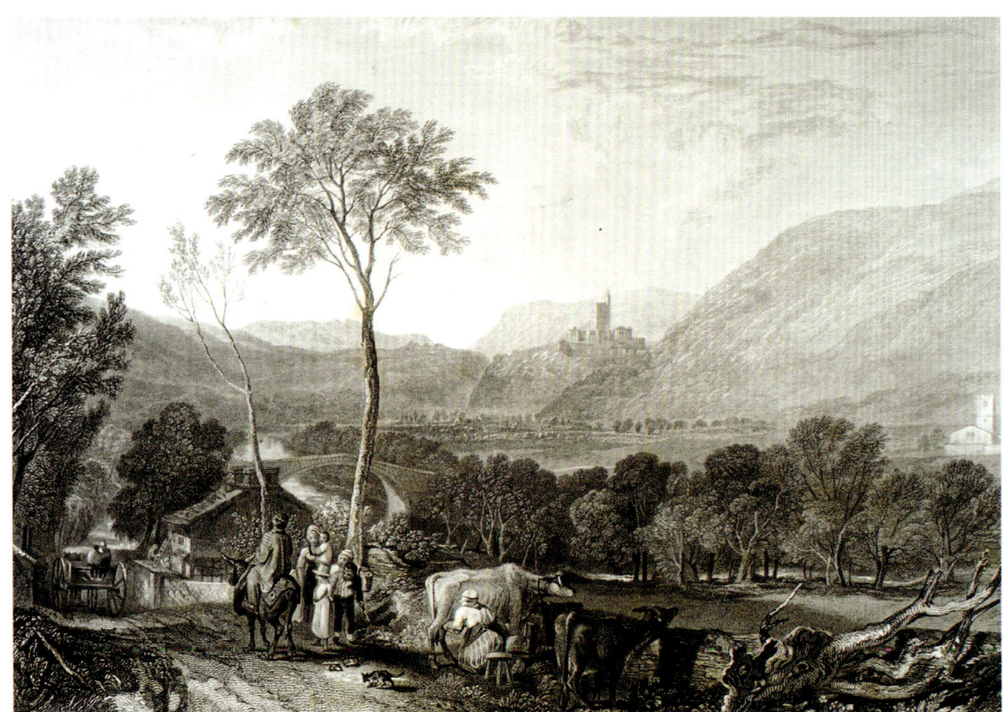

PLATE 32

Opposite

William Radclyffe

(1780 – 1855)

Hornby Castle from Tatham Church

Engraving after J. M. W. Turner

The Bowes Museum

PLATE 33

Right

Hornby Castle

Contemporary photograph

Michael Rudd

THE TOPOGRAPHY IS ACCURATE, ALTHOUGH IT IS NECESSARILY COMPRESSED; THE ROADSIDE WALL AND TREES ARE STILL THERE, AS IS THE MEADOW NEXT TO THE RIVER. TODAY WE HAVE TO BE CONTENT WITH A DIFFERENT VIEW FROM THE BRIDGE OVER THE RIVER WENNING IN HORNBY.

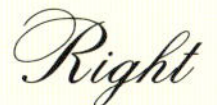

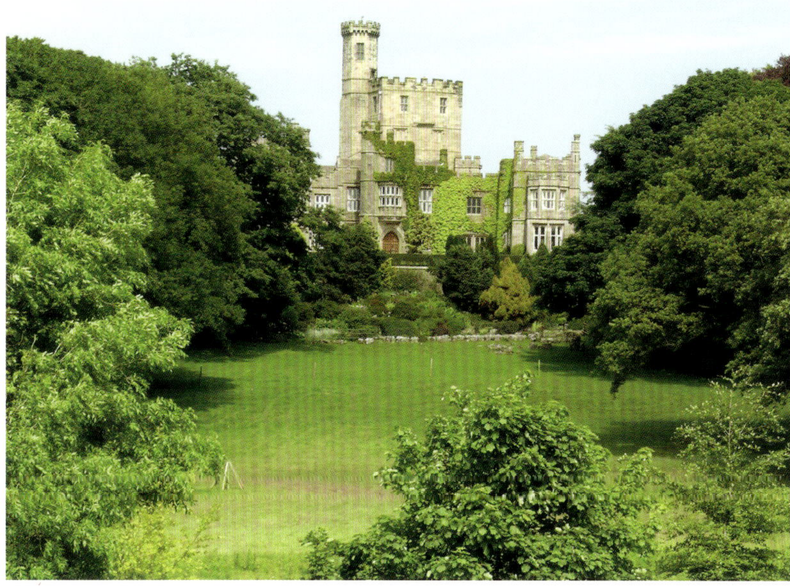

along the now dismantled railway, obviously not there in 1816, between the river and the road, obscure our view today. In following Turner along the road we too pass (next to a much more recent house) a cottage with its 1642 date stone, the Bridge Inn dated 1744 and the buildings opposite. A little above the inn we easily find the spot where Turner chose to make a detailed study in his *Yorkshire 4* sketchbook [CXLVII 41a].[30] Despite the growth of trees, the rebuilding of the bridge, the remains of the railway and the addition of a few more buildings, the scene is quite well preserved.

From just above the Bridge Inn Turner recorded the road passing the inn and leading the eye over the bridge to the castle beyond; Tatham church appears on the right-hand edge of the page. In the watercolour Turner follows his notes on the sketch to depict the 'River sparkling among the trees', these being 'alders'; he retains the two foreground trees and adds a wealth of activity in the road beside the 'meadow'.

Part of the wall in front of the inn and cottage remains, although not the two smaller buildings, one with entrance door; the low building opposite is visible too. The cottage has retained the distinctive chimney merely indicated in the sketch but perfectly recalled in the watercolour.

Perhaps because of the weather conditions, Turner did not seem satisfied with his sketch of the castle, as he returned to Hornby to make closer studies[31] which he later used in the watercolour. Today we have to be content with a different view from the bridge over the River Wenning in Hornby.

Turner then rode to Kirkby Lonsdale and the Sun Inn. After making further sketches at Kirkby Lonsdale, the Ingleborough area and Skipton, he would reach Farnley Hall on 11 August.

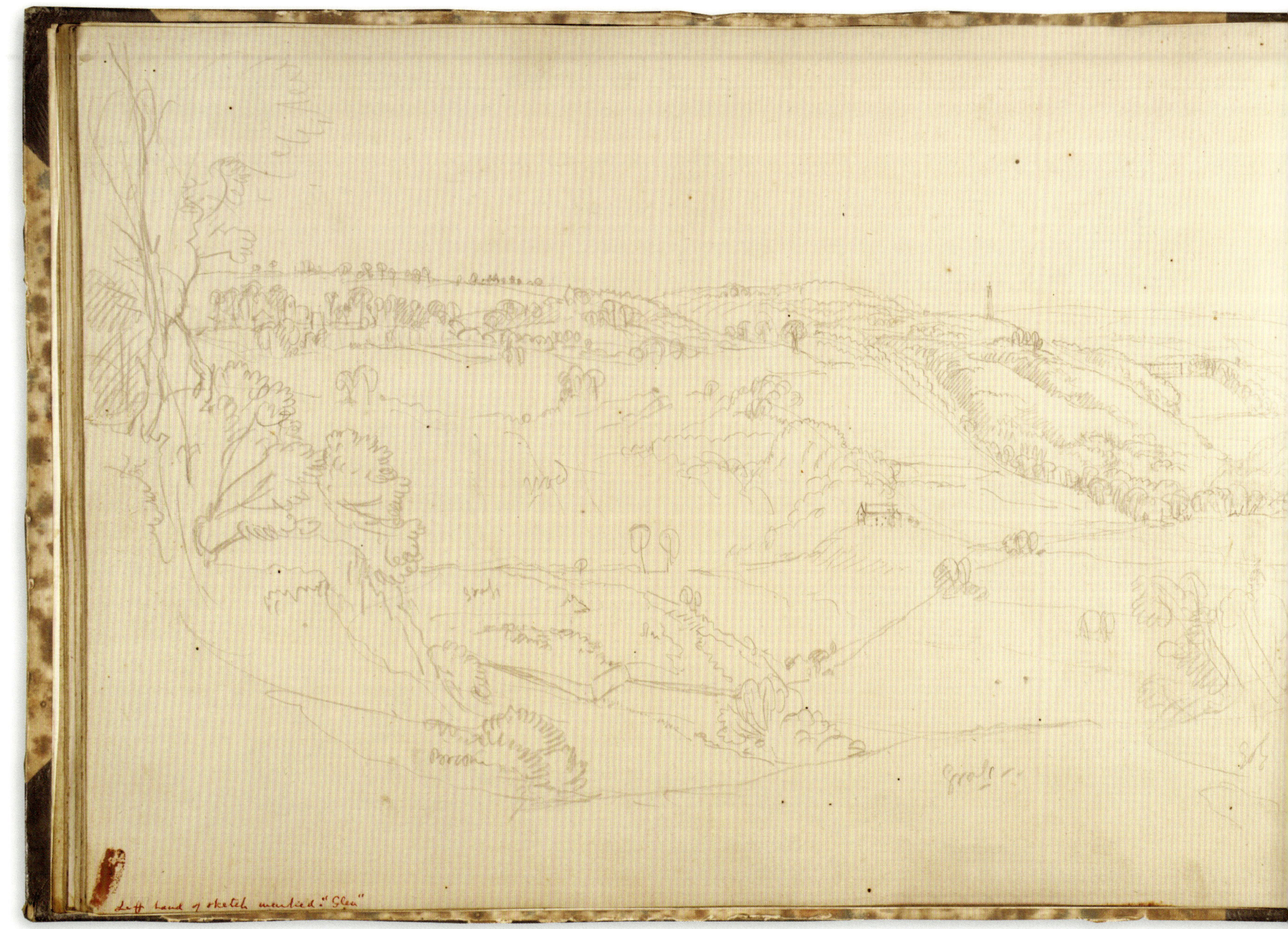

PLATE 34

J. M. W. Turner, *Gibside from the South*, 1817, Raby Sketchbook
Tate, bequeathed by the artist 1856

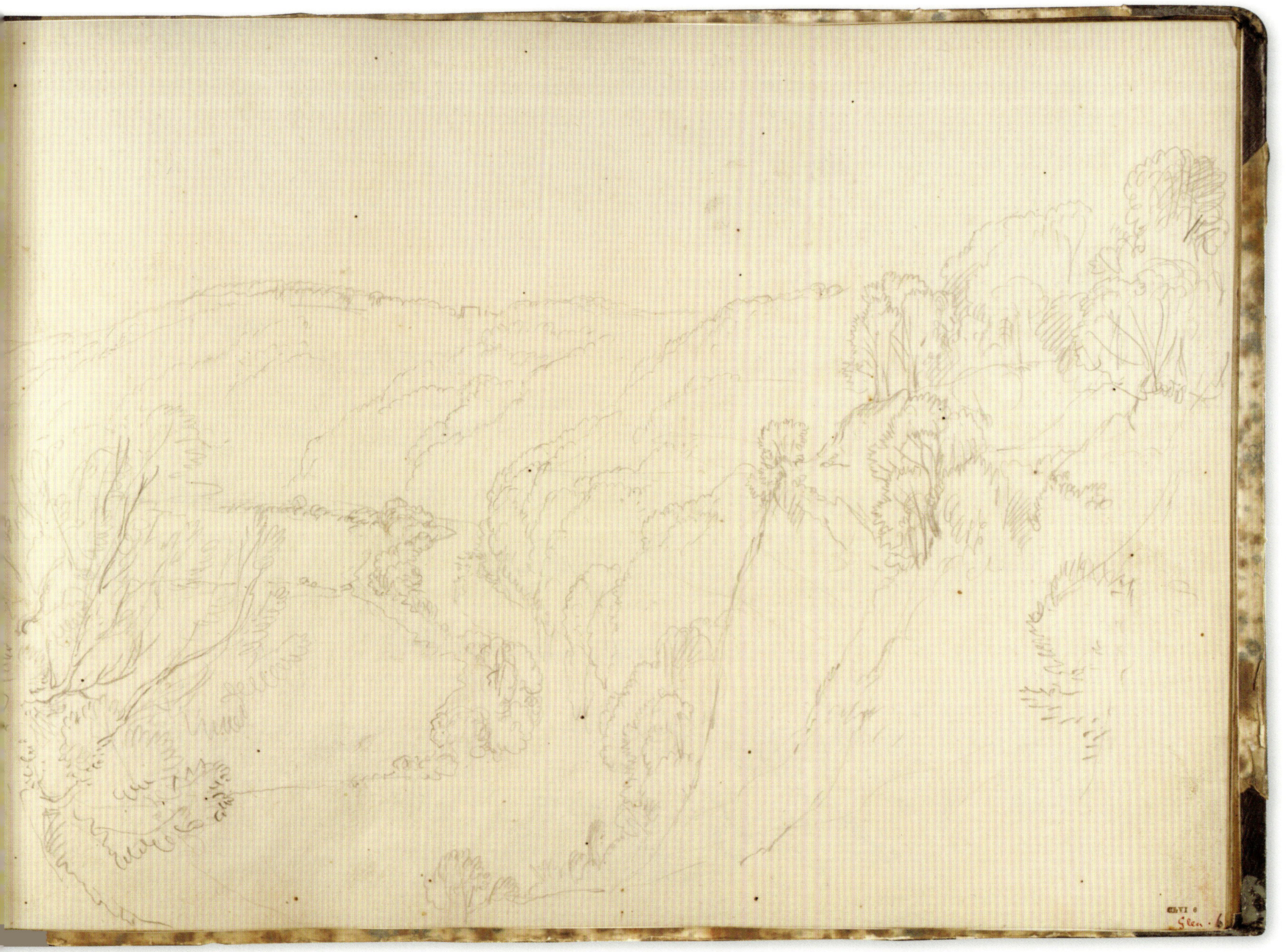

1817

Gibside

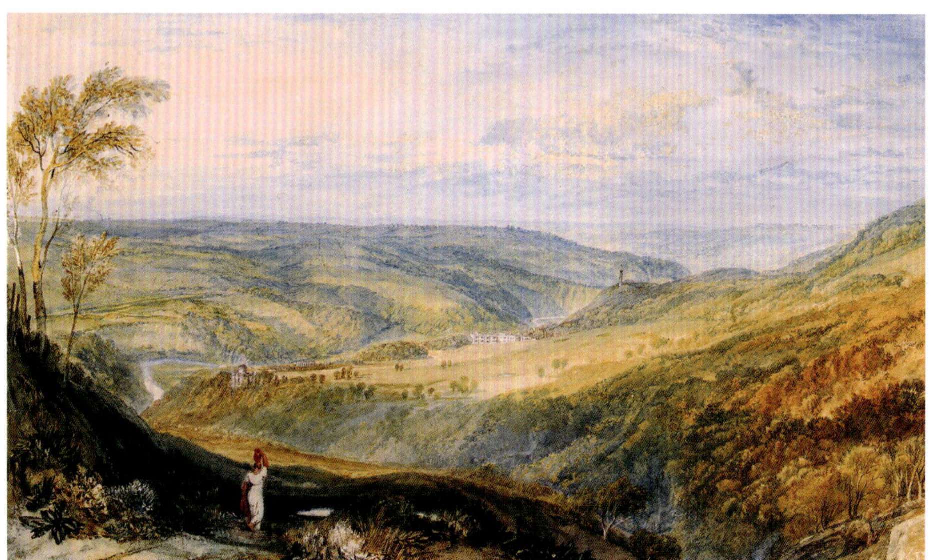

Gibside from the south

TURNER'S MAIN VIEWPOINT FROM THE SOUTH OF GIBSIDE, at Bryan's Leap, is still recognisable today [CLVI 3v – 4]. The foreground was sketched (plate 34) from about 250 metres lower down the slope; it was only when investigating this that I discovered the stone steps shown by Turner, now hidden by vegetation. While he was sketching on Sandy Path Lane here, Turner seems, from a figure and a note on his sketch, to have been passed by a 'child carrying water'; in the same position on the watercolour he painted a woman with a jar on her head descending these steps. From the way she is dressed in classical drapery, holding her dress over her left arm, it may be that this figure is based on, or refers us to, that on top of the Column to Liberty in the park. This would have appealed to Turner's decidedly libertarian leanings.

This column, over forty-five metres high, was built as an expression of George Bowes' wealth and influence; by 1759 the final cost was £1,601 18s. 9¾d.[32] For the top of the column Bowes finally chose the figure of Liberty, complete with staff of maintenance and cap of liberty, proclaiming his support for the Whig party.

PLATE 35

Opposite

J. M. W. Turner

Gibside, County Durham, The Seat of The Earl of Strathmore

circa 1817

Watercolour on paper

The Bowes Museum

PLATE 36

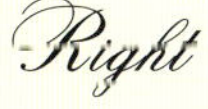

Samuel Rawle

(1771 – 1860)

Gibside, County Durham, The Seat of The Earl of Strathmore

1819

Engraving after J. M. W. Turner

The Bowes Museum

WHEN ENGRAVING THE WATERCOLOUR, SAMUEL RAWLE, ON TURNER'S INSTRUCTION, HAS ADDED THE FIGURE OF A CHILD WALKING BESIDE THE WOMAN CARRYING A JAR ON HER HEAD; WAS THIS A REFERENCE TO THE ARTIST'S NOTE ON HIS SKETCH, 'CHILD CARRYING WATER'?

From left to right in the sketch, we note the chapel, the walled garden with garden house, the Long Walk, Gibside House, and the Column to Liberty. Turner records two patches of 'water', fields of 'turnip' and 'corn', 'Beech Wood' and the 'wall'; the wall just features on the extreme right of the watercolour (plate 35), edging West Wood. Other features identifiable today include the farm in the Leap Mill Burn valley, complete with smoke curling upwards and with its barn roof timbers exposed in 1817; and the crags and road above the River Derwent. Just to the left of the Column to Liberty Turner shows Scar Bank and Winlaton Bank above the river; it was from this viewpoint that he made his other major two-page sketch of Gibside. The railway, with the nine arched viaduct still visible, was built in 1867 along the Derwent valley but avoiding most of the Gibside estate.

The area of water in the Parkfields of Gibside fed a fountain on the open ground in front of the Orangery. Trees along the Long Walk from the Chapel to the Column now prevent us seeing this Orangery, Gibside House, or Green Close (itself cleared of plantation in 2005).

In his sketch Turner spent some time detailing the fields, settlements and road to the north of the Derwent; of these there is little trace in the watercolour. However the trees and posts along with the steps and the steep bank on the extreme left are used, although a sapling and foreground plants are added. In the far right foreground Turner very lightly indicates a couple of roofs, with smoke rising slowly upwards; these could be associated with the Gibside quarries along the Leap Mill Burn valley. A careful examination of the watercolour reveals three areas of smoke rising from this small valley.

At one edge of his sketch of Gibside from the south, Turner has made four detailed studies. Here are the Column of Liberty, Gibside House with the recently constructed parapet, the Chapel and part of the Orangery. The latter is complete with hipped roof and the now missing urns on top of the balustrade; the artist only draws one of the arched bays of the front of this greenhouse and makes a note that this is one of seven; Turner's other note here may be deciphered as 'Part of Warm House'. These detailed drawings are easily verified on a visit to Gibside, where the House and Orangery are being conserved.

When engraving the watercolour, Samuel Rawle, on Turner's instruction, has added the figure of a child walking beside the woman carrying a jar on her head (plate 36); was this a reference to the artist's note on his sketch, 'child carrying water'?

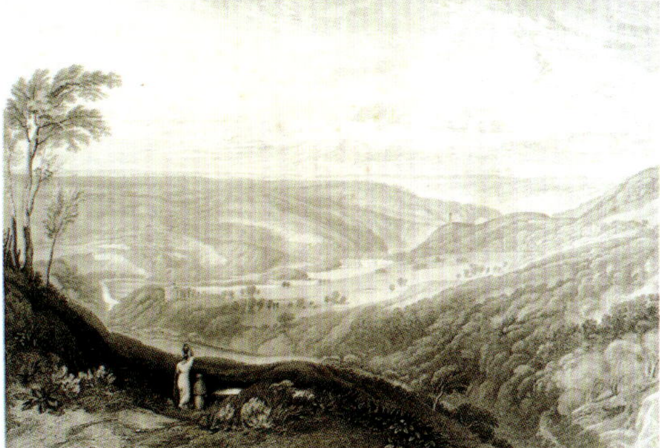

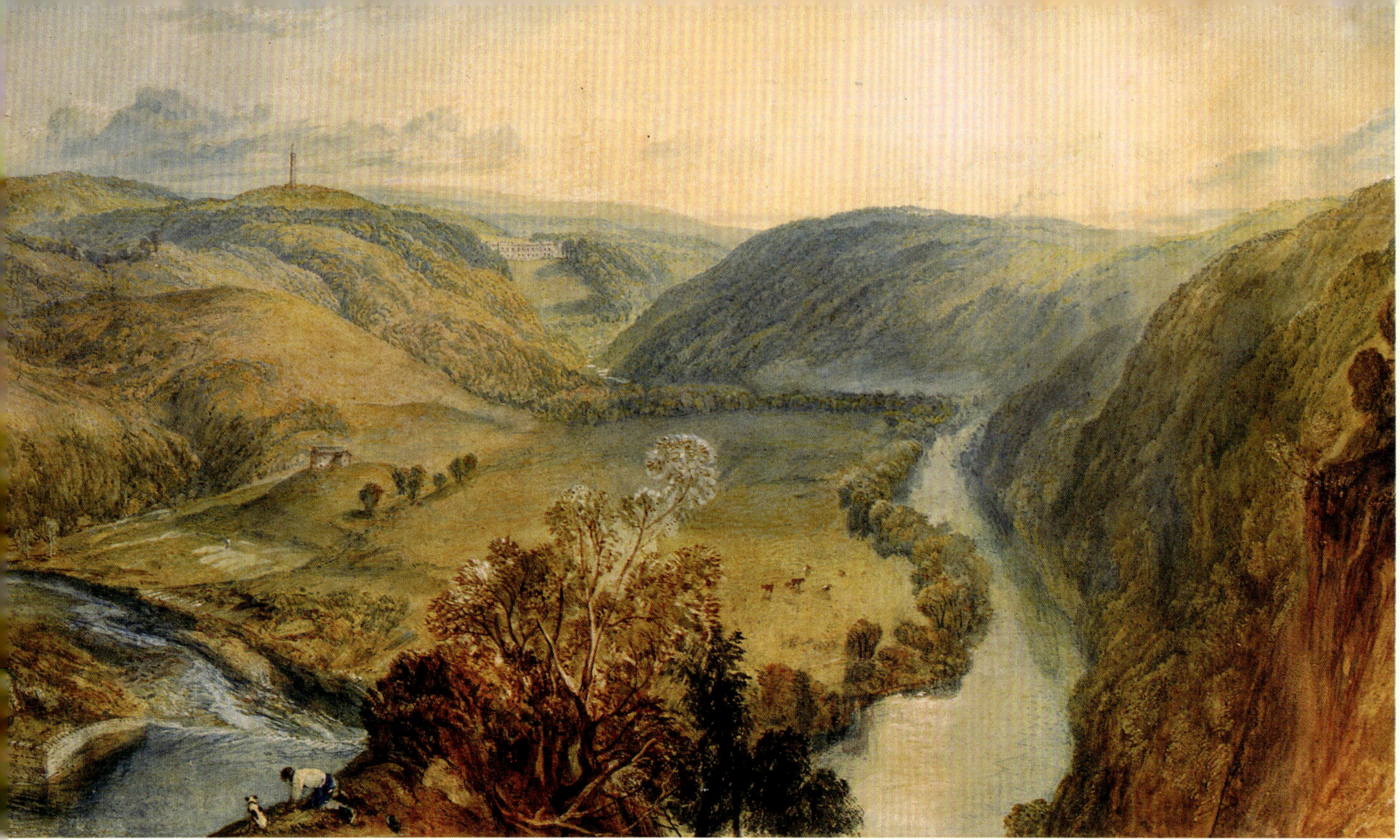

PLATE 37

Left

J. M. W. Turner

Gibside from the North

circa 1817

Watercolour on paper

The Bowes Museum

PLATE 38

Opposite

J. M. W. Turner

Barnard Castle

circa 1830 – 1831

Pencil on paper

Rokeby and Appleby sketchbook, Tate, bequeathed by the artist 1856

TURNER USED TWENTY-SEVEN PAGES IN HIS LARGE SKETCHBOOK AND FIFTEEN IN HIS POCKET-BOOK FOR THIS IMPORTANT COMMISSION AT RABY. THE BASIS OF THE ENGRAVING IS A DETAILED SKETCH OF THE CASTLE WITH FURTHER DETAILS TAKEN FROM BOTH SKETCHBOOKS.

Gibside from the north

FOR THIS VIEW TURNER USED TWO FULL PAGES of his *Raby* sketchbook [CLVI 5a – 6]. Despite the growth of trees, Turner's viewpoint part way down Winlaton Scar can still be identified, looking down over Goodshields Haugh. The foreground shows the steep 'scar' where the River Derwent erodes the boulder clay-topped river cliffs; in the centre foreground Turner shows his actual viewpoint – a tree's roots help to prevent a portion of cliff from being cut away. As well as the Column to Liberty and Gibside House, Turner carefully sketches the weir or High Dam with its Slitting Mill Race constructed around 1697 (and rebuilt in 1760) to lead water into Ambrose Crowley's Winlaton Ironworks further north.

Although Turner sketches the fourteenth century fortified Hollinside Manor acquired by George Bowes in 1730, when compressing the scene for his watercolour (plate 37) this feature had to be omitted.

When comparing the present-day middleground of Goodshields Haugh with the sketch, recourse had to be made to the first edition Ordnance Survey map of 1857, as this area was landscaped in the 1990s after colliery waste was deposited here. The pattern of field boundaries and trees matches the sketch, and where Turner indicates a cottage, the map indicates 'old walls' with a track from Hollinside.

Raby

For the important commission at Raby Turner used twenty-seven pages in his large sketchbook and fifteen in his pocket-book. The basis of the engraving is a detailed sketch of the castle [CLVI 19a], plus another[33] showing the main grouping of dogs, huntsmen and stags in relation to an outline of the castle. Details are taken from both sketchbooks; for example, in the pocket-book there are five of hounds with their individual markings and names [CLIX 63]; some of these[34] can be related directly to the engraving. On one page[35] Turner appears to have ticked the sketch of the particular huntsman he intends to use in his watercolour.

The main sketch unusually contains a number of figures. In the engraving a figure in a doorway is retained from the sketch, as well as two of the three figures walking in front of the castle, although in the engraving (plate 6) their position is changed and a dog joins them.

1830 to 1831

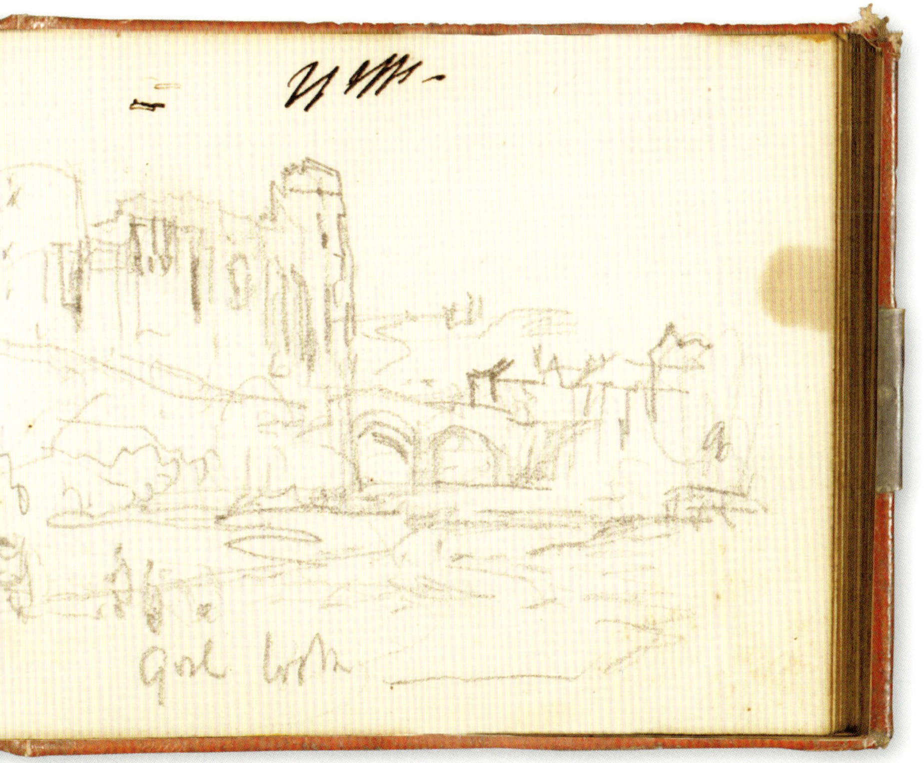

Turner revisited sites such as Rokeby, the junction of the Greta and Tees and Barnard Castle. The *Barnard Castle* study [CCLXIV 55a] (plate 38) in the *Rokeby and Appleby* sketchbook is from a similar viewpoint to those Turner had used in 1797 and 1816, although by now the building on the bridge over the river Tees had gone. Although very economical, this sketch still shows details such as the fifteenth century oriel window in the Great Chamber, and the windows and buttresses of the Great Hall.

Walking through the landscape Turner captured in his sketchbooks and later brought to life in his watercolours and engravings offers us an opportunity to reappraise his working process. Turner continued to refer to earlier sketchbooks and revisit earlier viewpoints throughout his career. In visiting the locations he recreated, we begin to understand how Turner manipulated the landscape around him to create his artworks.

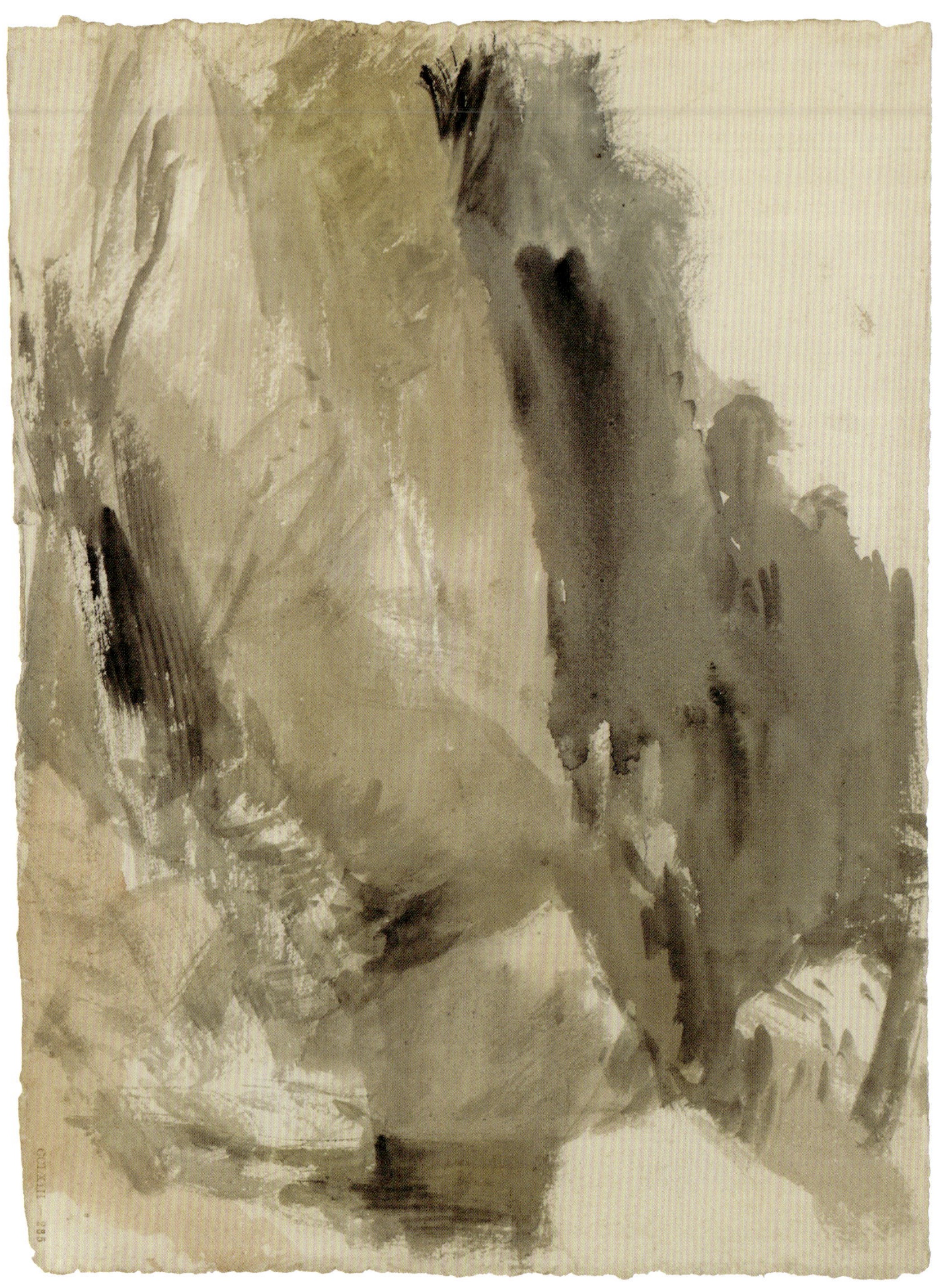

PLATE 39

Opposite

J. M. W. Turner

Study for 'Rokeby'

1822

Watercolour on paper

Tate,
bequeathed by the artist
1856

A PRÉCIS
of
TURNER'S WATERCOLOUR MATERIALS, TECHNIQUES *and* IDEAS

by Paul Clark

THE PAINTER AND DIARIST JOSEPH FARINGTON (1747–1821) recorded on 21 July 1799 that Turner called on him during the morning. The same day, Hoppner held a tea party in the garden of his Fulham home, attended by fellow artists and academicians Opie, Fuseli and Sawrey Gilpin. Turner joined them later and during a conversation with Farington, gave a hint about how he produced his watercolours:

> *He told me he has no systematic process for making drawings. He avoids any particular mode that he may not fall into manner. By washing and occasionally rubbing out he at last expresses in some degree the idea in his mind.*[1]

Turner called on Farington again a few months later, on 16 November 1799, and, still pursuing the same method:

> *He reprobated the mechanically systematic process of drawing practised by Smith* [John Smith, known as 'Warwick Smith'] *and from him so generally diffused. He thinks it can produce nothing but manner and sameness. The practice of* [here a blank is discreetly left] *is still more vicious. Turner has no settled process but drives the colours about till he has expressed the idea in his mind.*[2]

If the above epitomises Turner's early watercolour practice, then some thirty-seven years later the artist W. L. Leitch provides us with a most vivid insight into Turner's almost production-line methods of watercolour painting. Recollecting from a visit to his studio he states:

> *There were four drawing boards, each of which had a handle screwed to the back. Turner, after sketching the subject in a fluent manner, grasped the handle and plunged the whole drawing into a pail of water by his side. Then quickly he washed in the principal hues that he required, flowing tint into tint, until this stage of the work was complete. Leaving this drawing to dry, he took a second board and repeated the operation. By the time the fourth drawing was laid in, the first would be ready for the finishing touches.*
>
> *Turner's method was to float the broken colours, while the paper was wet, while several of his water-colours were in progress at the same time. He stretched the paper on boards and plunging them into water, he dropped the colours onto the paper while it was wet, making marblings and gradations throughout the work. His completing process was marvellously rapid for he indicated*

his masses and incidents, took out half-lights and dragged, hatched and stippled until the design was finished. This swiftness, grounded on the scale practiced in early life, enabled Turner to preserve the purity and luminosity of his work and to paint at a prodigiously rapid rate.[3]

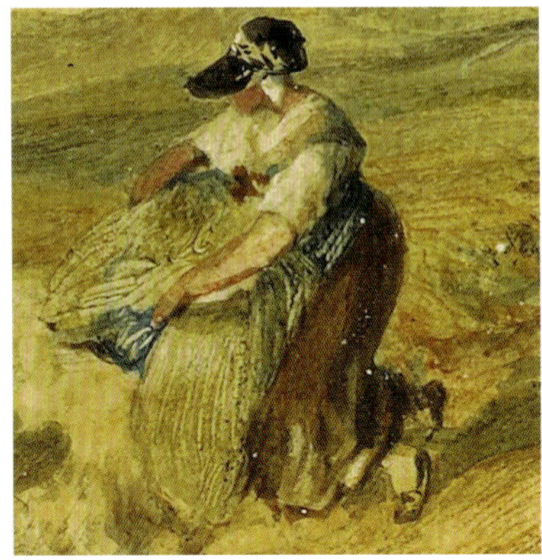

The process to which Leitch refers evolved from Turner's youthful practice of laying in and building up an image with successive tints of watercolour – particularly in architectural and topographical subjects – beginning with the lightest and most translucent, through to the mid tones and onto the darkest colours. He thus learnt the power of tone and how it could produce a sense of immense depth and contrast on a small scale.

Washing dry watercolour paint, to fade it, with a wet brush or sponge will achieve variations of tone and expose undertints to create finely dissolving distances and textural effects in, for example, foregrounds, terrain and masonry.

Dragging colour is achieved by loading the brush with wet paint and half drying the bristles on a piece of cloth, then skimming the surface of the paper, leaving dry particles of colour on top of base tints to create, for example, effects of rippling water, foliage, landscape details and other areas of form which need to be indicated in relief.

Stipple and hatching can look like finely chopped straw and involves the use of a wet or semi-dry brush to paint crisp sharp lines, rather like a sharp HB pencil, in order to build up details, indicate form, structure or direction in atmospheric effects.

Highlights may be pulled out of wet or dry paint with the point of a damp brush; a sharp edge or fingernail could also be employed. Lead white and chalk were also used in the same vein and could also be mixed with coloured pigment to create bodycolour. Gouache can be made with pure coloured pigment and opaque white to achieve the force and power of oil paint if used with skill and sensitivity – a technique that will be referred to in turn.

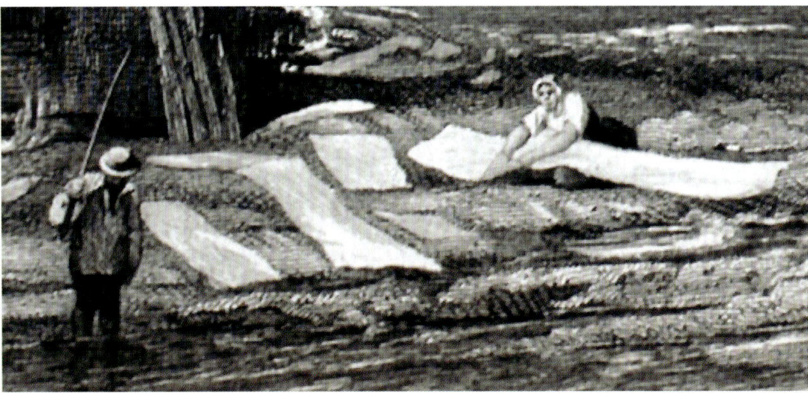

PLATE 40

Left, top

Detail

J. M. W. Turner

Heysham and Cumberland Mountains

1818

Watercolour with some scraping-out on paper

The British Museum

PLATE 41

Left, bottom

Detail

T. Higham

Eggleston Abbey, near Barnard Castle

Engraving, after J. M. W. Turner

The Bowes Museum

PLATE 42

Opposite

J. M. W. Turner

Richmond, Yorkshire, Sunrise: Colour Study

1799

Watercolour on paper

Tate, bequeathed by the artist 1856

Paper

Tough sheets of paper were required to produce watercolours that contained such complex and robust techniques. Different papers produce different visual effects when used for watercolour painting. The papers, like the paint and the artist's skill, set limits to what can and cannot be done in the medium.[4] Fortunately for Turner and other artists in the late eighteenth and nineteenth centuries, there was a whole range of good quality handmade, linen rag based, gelatine sized and bleach free papers available, made by the likes of Whatman, Bally Ellen and Steart, and Portals, among others. Many of their papers were designed for writing on; their tough surface texture could withstand abrasive pen nibs and were therefore eminently suitable for the rigours of watercolour painting. Such papers enabled Turner to produce a range of effects in the medium from simple washes of paint to highly detailed brilliantly complex work.[5]

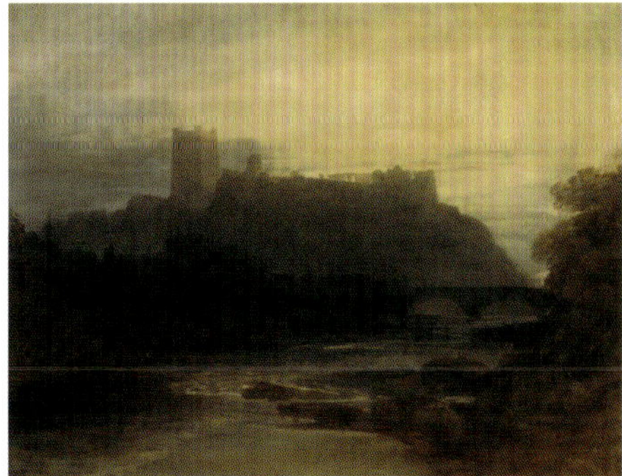

Watercolour Paints

Watercolour paints and recipes from eighteenth and nineteenth century colourmen such as Rudolph Ackermann, Reeves, Robertson, Winsor and Newton, the analysis of paint samples, and my own comparative experiments reveal a whole range of gums, plus plasticizers, honey and sugar candy, present in Turner's (and other artists') paint samples, mediums and finished works.[6] Gums that can be found include arabic (*Acacia* species), cherry (*Prunus* species), tragacanth (*Astragalus* species), and their relatives. This is important because different gums, when used as pigment binders, produce different watercolour paint films, from matt, eggshell to glossy. They can also produce different textures, from the thick and inert to the thin and soluble. The paint's colour tone, ranging from the brilliant and luminous to the dull and flat, is influenced by the refractive index of the gums, sugars or other substances coating the pigment, or indeed, by their absence.[7] The use of plasticizers, such as honey or sugar candy, affects all of the above characteristics, in particular adhesion, solubility and colour tone. They have been replaced today, in the main, with glycerine and chemicals.

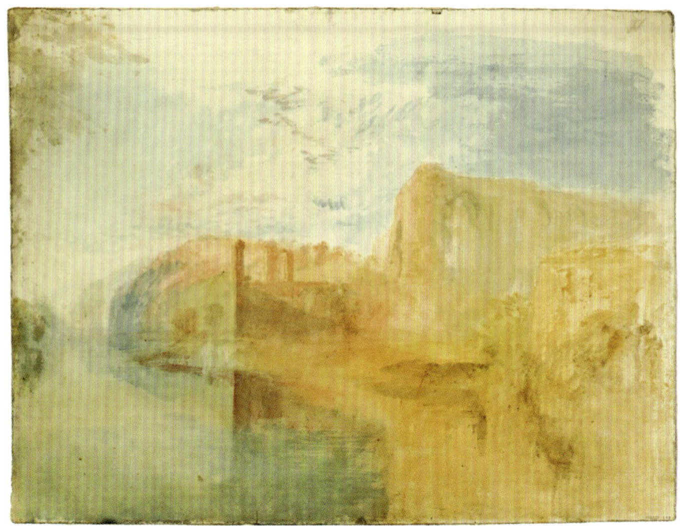

Recipes and ratios for binding watercolour cakes and liquid paints varied but more often than not *Acacia* gums were diluted one part to two, three, four and even more parts water. Plasticizers (sugar candy or honey) were added to help the paint flow and adhere, at anywhere between one-tenth to half a part ratio to gum. Sometimes only gum and water were used as a binder but, without plasticizers, they usually produced brittle paint films. On the other hand, the colourman Rudolph Ackerman experimented with pigments bound only with honey without gum. However, without the latter, they could lift up easily from the paper's surface.

Many other gums and substances found their way into watercolour paint recipes, sometimes by default, being mistaken for *Acacias*, whilst some artists and colourmen experimented with various species such as cherry gum, or *sarcocolla*, because of their different qualities of viscosity and adhesion.

Gum tragacanth was recommended as a gouache binder because of its reputation for absorbing powdery substances and keeping them in an even suspension (both bodycolour and gouache often incorporated powdery chalk or an opaque white such as lead white in their recipe). Tragacanth produced very matt paint films if used on its own, needing plasticizers or other gums to help it flow from the brush and onto the paper more easily.

The amount of pigment to binder obviously varied from colourmen or artists' preparation. This can be considered as a broad guide: approximately 30 to 40% for ultramarine, cobalts, yellow and iron oxides; 20 to 30% for Prussian blues, red iron oxides and most synthetic pigments; and 10 to 20% for strongly tinting dye-like pigments, such as Alizarin crimson.

In addition, many of the pigments Turner and other late eighteenth and nineteenth century artists used such as genuine ultramarine (*lapis lazuli*), certain Prussian and cobalt blues, chrome yellows, reds, madders, earth colours and lead white have now been substituted by synthetic dye based pigments which can give different paint film effects from those of Turner's era.

PLATE 43

Opposite

J. M. W. Turner

St. Agatha's Abbey, Easby, Yorkshire: colour study

circa 1820

Watercolour on paper

Tate,
bequeathed by the artist
1856

There was certainly nothing to prevent Turner or other artists from preparing gums to make their own paints or modifying commercial paints on the palette, or even using no gum at all in some instances, for example powdered pigment and water for a dilute translucent glaze.[8] We do know Turner sometimes used small jars of soluble paint, possibly bodycolour or gouache, into which he would dip brush or pen. This provided another opportunity to modify or temper paint with other substances as he saw fit.

From the above we can safely assume different media produce different pictorial effects, especially in the hands of different artists, each with their own technical skill and vision to transmit. Throughout the eighteenth and nineteenth centuries, many artists, not least Turner, attempted to capture qualities attributed to oil painting and transpose them to the watercolour medium and vice versa. John Gage, in his book *Colour in Turner; Poetry and Truth*, noted 'Turner's watercolour technique in the early 1830s certainly seems to have been affected by his experience of early Italian tempera painting'.[9]

Tempera painting may be considered as a bridge between water based and oil media, often borrowing and blending media attributed to both, such as gums, resins, eggs and oils. However, perhaps the greatest essay on achieving the force and power of oil paint in the watercolour medium is by Turner's greatest interpreter, John Ruskin, in the pages of his book *The Elements of Drawing*. Ruskin especially believed that the answer lay in a combination of dead colour, such as gouache or bodycolour with transparent watercolour.[10] These employed a water soluble based vehicle rather than an oil or varnish medium to whose glossy effects he was vehemently opposed. Ruskin stated:

> *After many years' study of the various results of fresco and oil painting in Italy, and of bodycolour and transparent colour in England, I am now entirely convinced that the greatest things that are to be done in art must be done in dead colour. The habit of depending on varnish or on lucid tints for transparency makes the painter comparatively lose sight of the nobler translucence which is obtained by breaking various colours amidst each other.*[11]

As the above hopefully demonstrates, technical and material secrets can be revealed through the research and analysis of an artist's work. This information may produce signposts to help other artists develop their own style or to forge their own track of truth. However, the most valuable essence of the picture making and creative process must remain as indefinable as some of the colour tones in Turner's works. Nevertheless Turner left us a major clue to the secrets of his success in the watercolour medium in the following, when Jane Fawkes pressed him, perhaps further than many would have dared, to reveal his secrets:

> *One of Mr. Fawkes' daughters told me* [W. L. Leitch] *that she was copying one of Turner's drawings and had a great deal of difficulty with one part of it. Her father saw how worried she was about it and said, 'Jane, don't fret your life out about that drawing. You are going up to London in a day or two; you are taking Mr. Turner his box of game and ever so many things; just take them to him yourself and give my kind compliments, and ask him as a great favour to tell you his secret for doing this.' So 'Jane' went with her good gifts, and was shown into the dull, dismal parlour, and then she gave her father's message. Turner answered her, 'Make my kindest respects to Mr. Fawkes, and tell him that the only secret I have got is d___d hard work.' Not deterred by this, she ventured to ask him another question. There were some very curious lights on the edges of some leaves in the drawing, and she begged him to tell her how they were done. 'Keep it all wet, and go that way,' said he, jerking about with his thumbnail.*[12]

TURNER *and* THE ART *of*

ENGRAVING

by Emma House

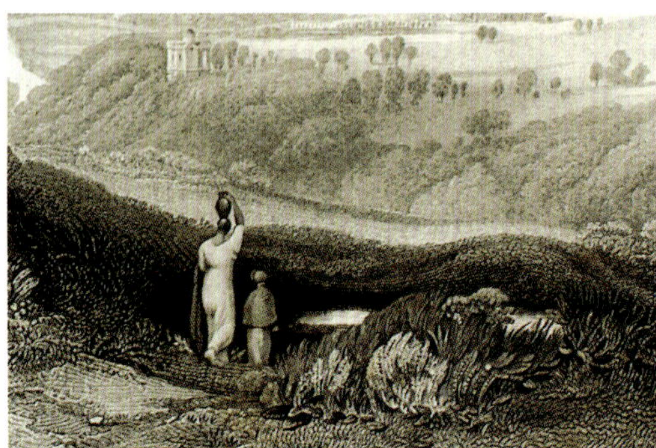

ALTHOUGH TURNER EXHIBITED AT THE ROYAL ACADEMY throughout his life, as well as his own London Gallery, it was through the printed form that he reached new and varied audiences, introducing his work to the majority of society. As a child, John Ruskin (1819–1900) received a copy of Samuel Rogers's *Italy*. This treasured birthday gift provided Ruskin with his first opportunity to study the work of Turner at length. Ruskin acknowledged the influence the publication's engravings had on him as the catalyst for a lifelong immersion in fine art claiming 'I might... attribute to the gift the entire direction of my life's energies.'[1]

The prints produced from Turner's Northern subjects are among his most intricate and exquisite engravings. Working repeatedly with printed images and engravers at each stage of the proofing process, Turner developed a skilful eye. For each design, he guided the engraver until the image they were working on resembled his watercolour, often surpassing it in beauty and form. It is a testimony to the skill and professionalism of line engravers that whilst Turner tried his hand at a number of printing processes, including etching and mezzotint, he always employed those proficient in the art form of line engraving to translate images into the engraved format.[2]

Turner's dedication to producing the highest quality engravings raised its status from a mere reproductive process to a highly skilled and collectable art form. His interest in engraving is perhaps due to his exposure, at a young age, to prints in the fashionable shop windows of Covent Garden.[3] Under the employment of John Raphael Smith he hand coloured prints, and learnt the process and terminology of the printmaker.[4]

Turner inscribed the verso of the chalk drawing *Study of the Head and Torso of the Apollo Belvedere*, around 1792, with notes describing a method for preparing copper plates. Although the inscription is undated, it could be surmised that it dates from the same period as the sketch and indicates Turner's early interest in printing.

PLATE 44

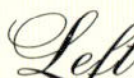

Left

Detail

Samuel Rawle

(1771 – 1860)

Gibside, County Durham, The Seat of The Earl of Strathmore

1819

Engraving
after J. W. M. Turner

The Bowes Museum

PLATE 45

Opposite

Detail

Samuel Rawle

(1771 – 1860)

Gibside, County Durham, The Seat of The Earl of Strathmore

Copper engraving plate
after J. W. M. Turner

The Earl of Strathmore & Kingthorne and County Durham County Record Office

WORKING REPEATEDLY WITH ENGRAVERS AT EACH STAGE OF THE PROOFING PROCESS, TURNER DEVELOPED A SKILFUL EYE. HE GUIDED THE ENGRAVER OF EACH DESIGN UNTIL THE IMAGE THEY WERE WORKING ON RESEMBLED HIS WATERCOLOUR, OFTEN SURPASSING IT IN BEAUTY AND FORM.

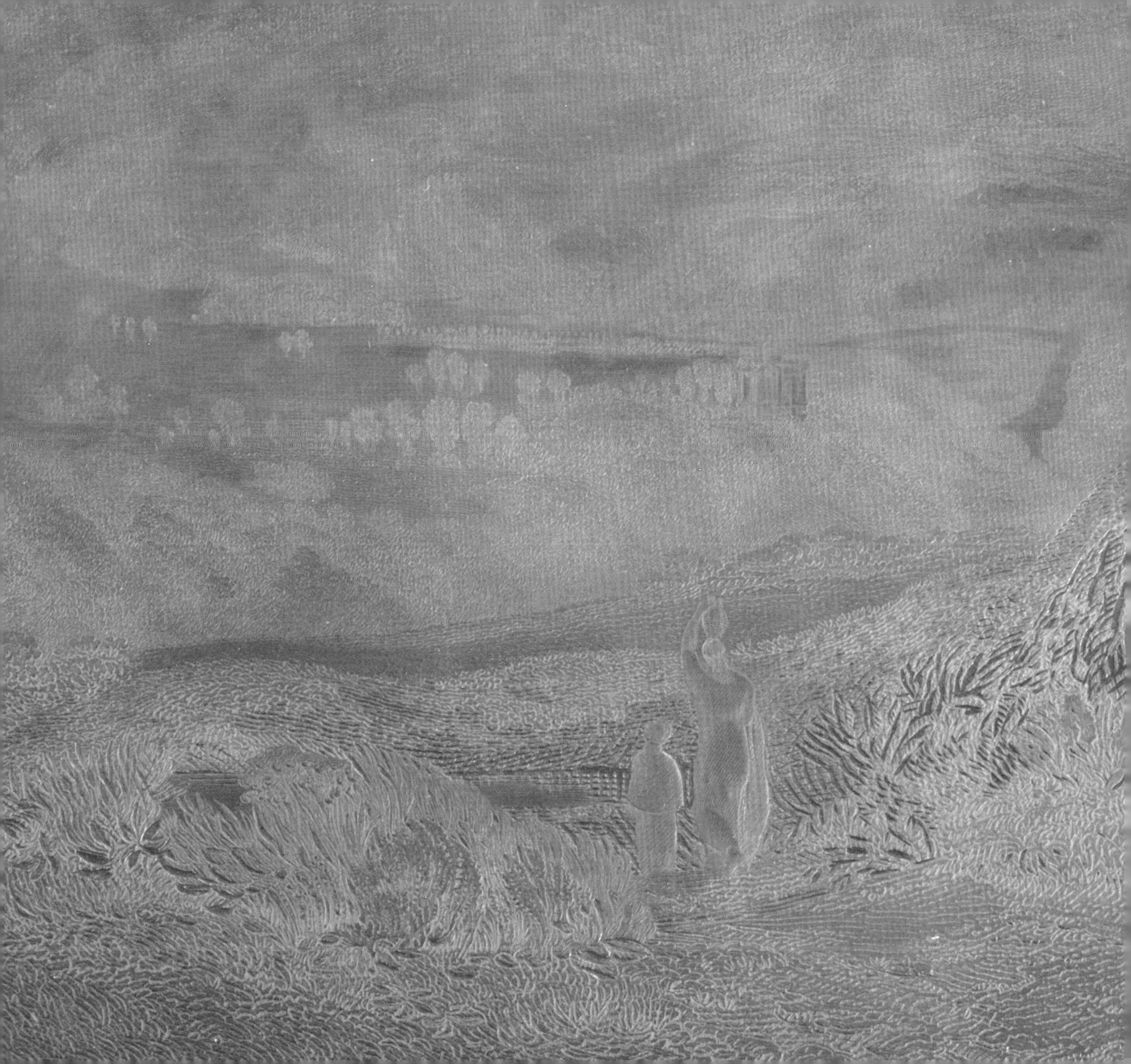

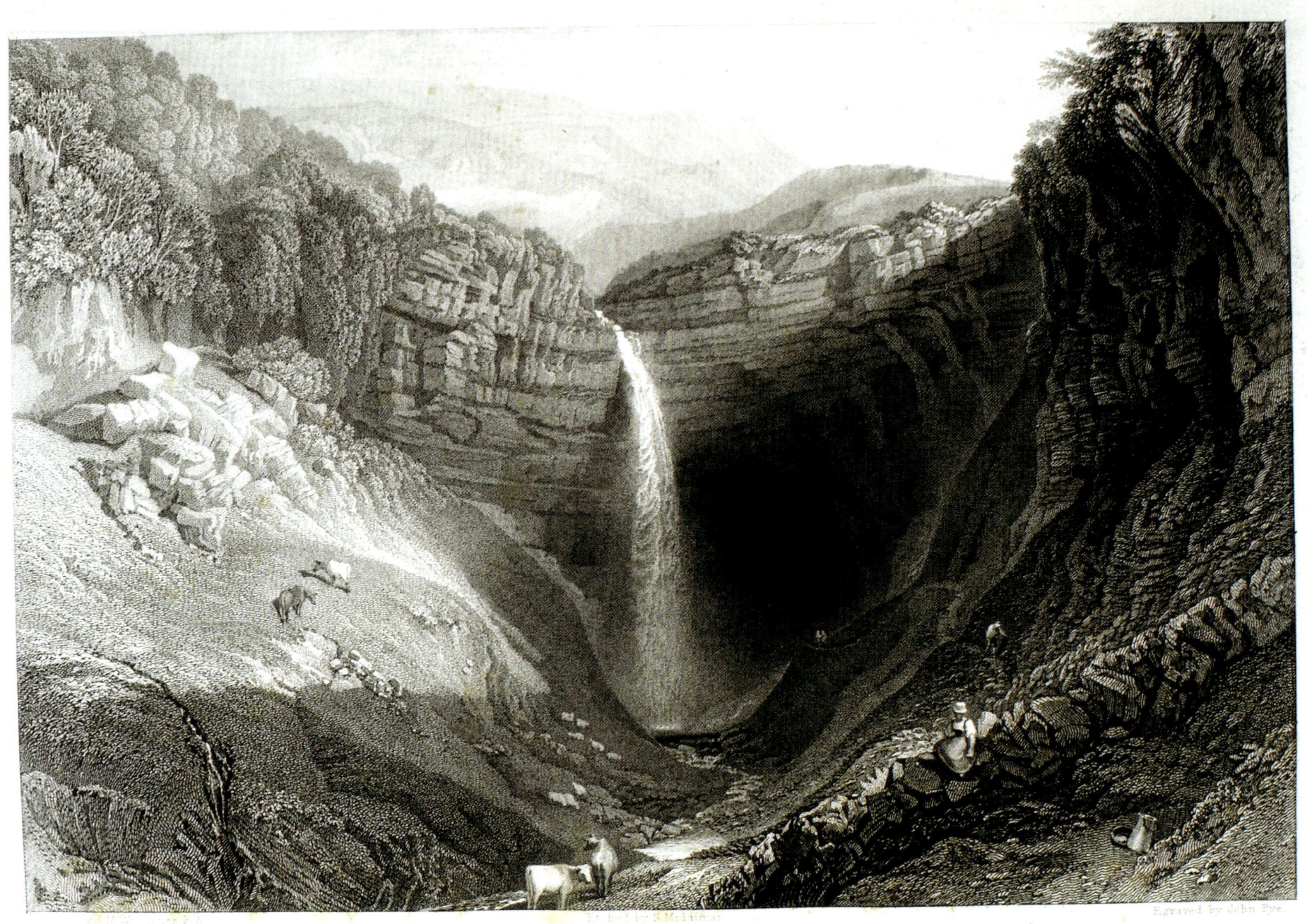

Etched by S. Middiman — Egraved by John Pye

Hardraw Fall.

PLATE 46

Opposite

S. Middiman

(1750 – 1831)

&

John Pye

(1782 – 1874)

Hardraw Fall

1818

Engraving
after J. M. W. Turner

The Bowes Museum

THE INTRICACIES AND ROUGH SURFACES OF THE GEOLOGICAL ROCK FORMATIONS IN THE ENGRAVINGS OF *HARDRAW FALL* ARE RENDERED EVEN MORE PERFECTLY THAN IN TURNER'S WATERCOLOUR.

ENGRAVING PRODUCTION

THE TERM ENGRAVING IS USED TO DESCRIBE the intaglio printing process where ink is transferred to paper from lines incised into a copper plate.[5] In the seventeenth century the introduction of etching in the initial stages of the production of engraving plates considerably reduced the long process, as the acid could make deeper furrows more quickly than an engraver.[6] Both etching and engraving processes were combined to produce the plates for Whitakers's *An History of Richmondshire*.[7]

The first step of the printing process would be to copy the outline of Turner's watercolour onto the copper plate in reverse. The image could then be etched onto the plate. The etching process involved covering the copper plate with a thin layer of ground (waxes and resins) and the details of the image were then scratched into the ground using a burin (sharp tool). The plate was then dipped in acid to eat away the exposed copper surface of the plate. The areas where the line should be less pronounced, such as in background details, were then stopped out (varnished over) which created a barrier between the acid and the copper plate. The whole plate was then dipped into the acid again.[8] This process was repeated a number of times allowing for deep lines in some areas, whilst others remained very fine.

The line engraver could then sharpen up the lines and differentiate the depth of scoring even further, by increasing grooves with a burin or by smoothing out furrows with a burnisher. The engraving was sometimes by another hand, as the inscription on *Hardraw Fall* (plate 46) indicates, as the two techniques required different skills.[9]

The minute differences in depth of scratching and scoring into the copper plate, which can be seen in the engraving plate *Gibside, County Durham* (plate 45), allowed a varying degree of ink to adhere to the plate.[10]

When the plates were freshly engraved, the deeply carved lines acted as reservoirs allowing the ink to flow into them. The first prints from the plate were printed onto fine quality India paper and the minute variations in ink allowed the printed image to take on an eloquence of light and dark unknown in any other printed form. These subtle differences allowed for every detail to convey texture on the paper. For example, the stonework of a ruined abbey is rendered with rough edges, whilst the billowing fabric of a farm worker's skirt is portrayed with a few lines. The subtleties of Turner's watercolour techniques translate seamlessly into the printed image. Turner, who commented on every engraved plate at each stage of its production, painstakingly controlled this process. The engravers would send proofs to Turner who would annotate them with diagrams and shading to indicate areas that should be changed or developed further. He sharpened his skills as he proofed each impression and developed a superior understanding of the quality and beauty that the printed medium could achieve.

An Artist's Eye

The methodical progression with which Turner and his engravers worked is illustrated by two engraver's proofs of *Junction of the Greta and the Tees at Rokeby* in the British Museum. The earlier proof (plate 47) depicts the plate before the details of the sky have been added and without the water rushing over the rocks in the foreground. The rocks have been built up with subtle furrows and grooves during the etching process, which gives them a dense form and texture. The area where water is later to be applied on the surface of the plate has remained covered with ground during etching and only a void indicates its role in the composition. Etchers worked skilfully, judging carefully the areas to be left blank and the details to etch to a lesser or greater degree. The etcher had to complete large amounts of work before a proof could be taken from the plate which would clearly indicate where further work was required. If the engraver had overworked the plate, areas could be smoothed by beating the plate from behind.

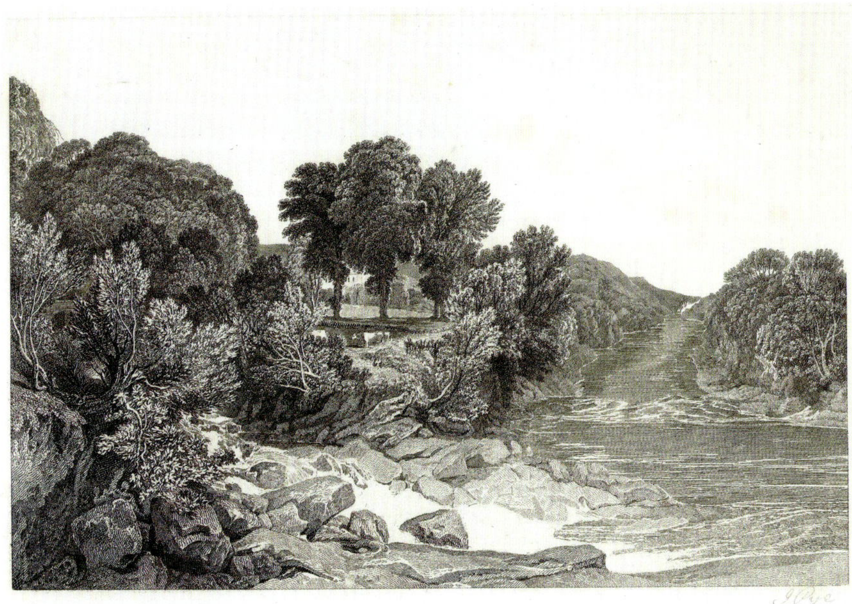

PLATE 47

Left

First Proof

John Pye

(1782 – 1874)

Junction of the Greta and the Tees at Rokeby

Engraving proof after J. M. W. Turner

The British Museum

PLATE 48

Opposite

Second Proof

John Pye

(1782 – 1874)

Junction of the Greta and the Tees at Rokeby

Engraving proof after J. M. W. Turner

The British Museum

The earlier proof, left, depicts the plate before the details of the water rushing over the rocks in the foreground have been added. The surface of the plate has remained covered with ground during etching and only a void indicates its role in the composition.

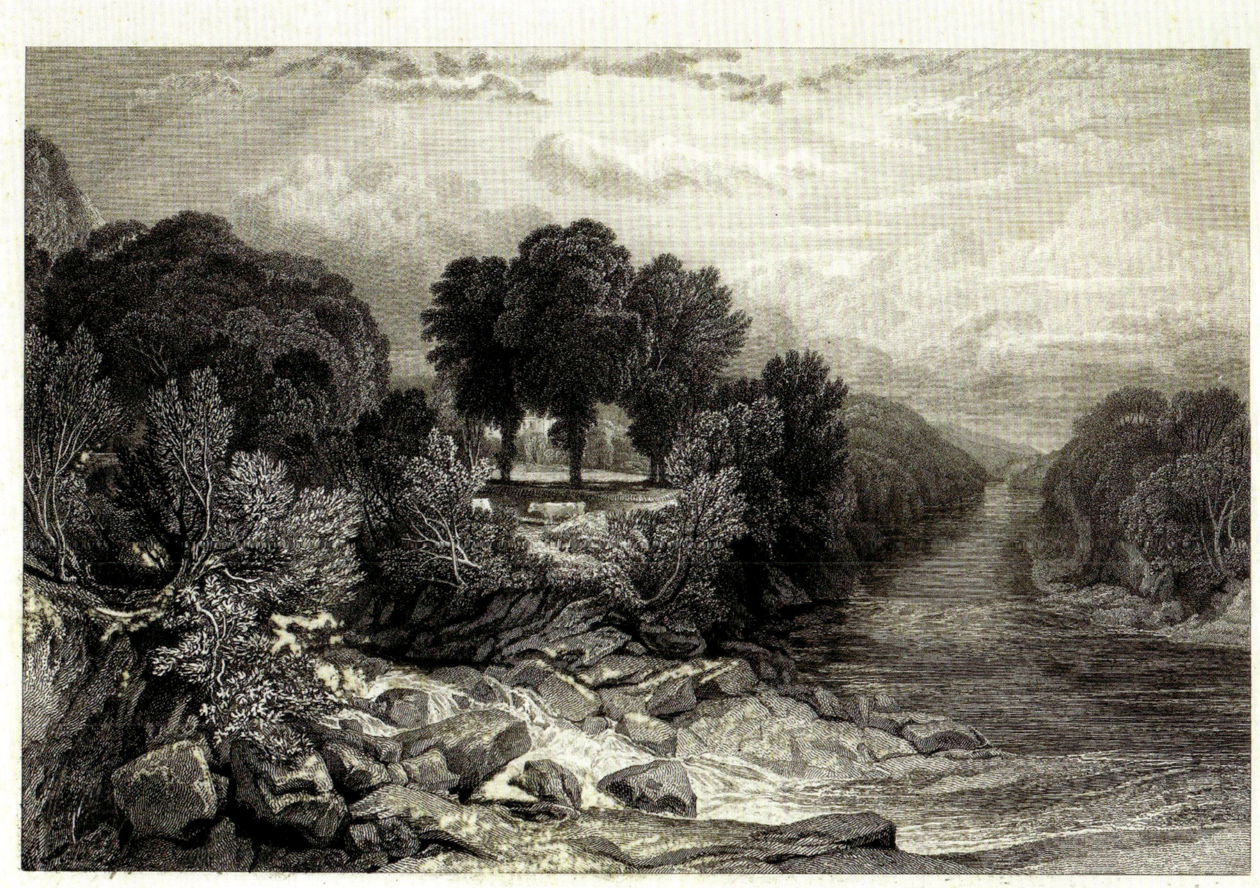

The later proof of *Junction of the Greta and the Tees at Rokeby* (plate 48) engraved by John Pye and touched by Turner in pencil is inscribed 'This proof touched by Turner is presented to C. Stokes Esq. Nov. 1857 John Pye'.[11] Where Turner desired a strengthening of shading in the shadows underneath the rocks in the foreground, he hatched a number of pencil lines. In the published image (plate 49) we can see the resulting cross hatching that Pye added to deepen the shadows under the rocks.

The development of the image is evident in the changes that occur to the engraving plate between the engraver's first and second proofs. In the first (plate 47) the arch of the bridge to the left of the image is plainly illustrated with horizontal lines. In the later touched proof (plate 48) Turner has pencilled in lines specifying the depiction of *voussoirs* (stones which form the arch of the bridge), which were then added and can be found in the final published image (plate 50).

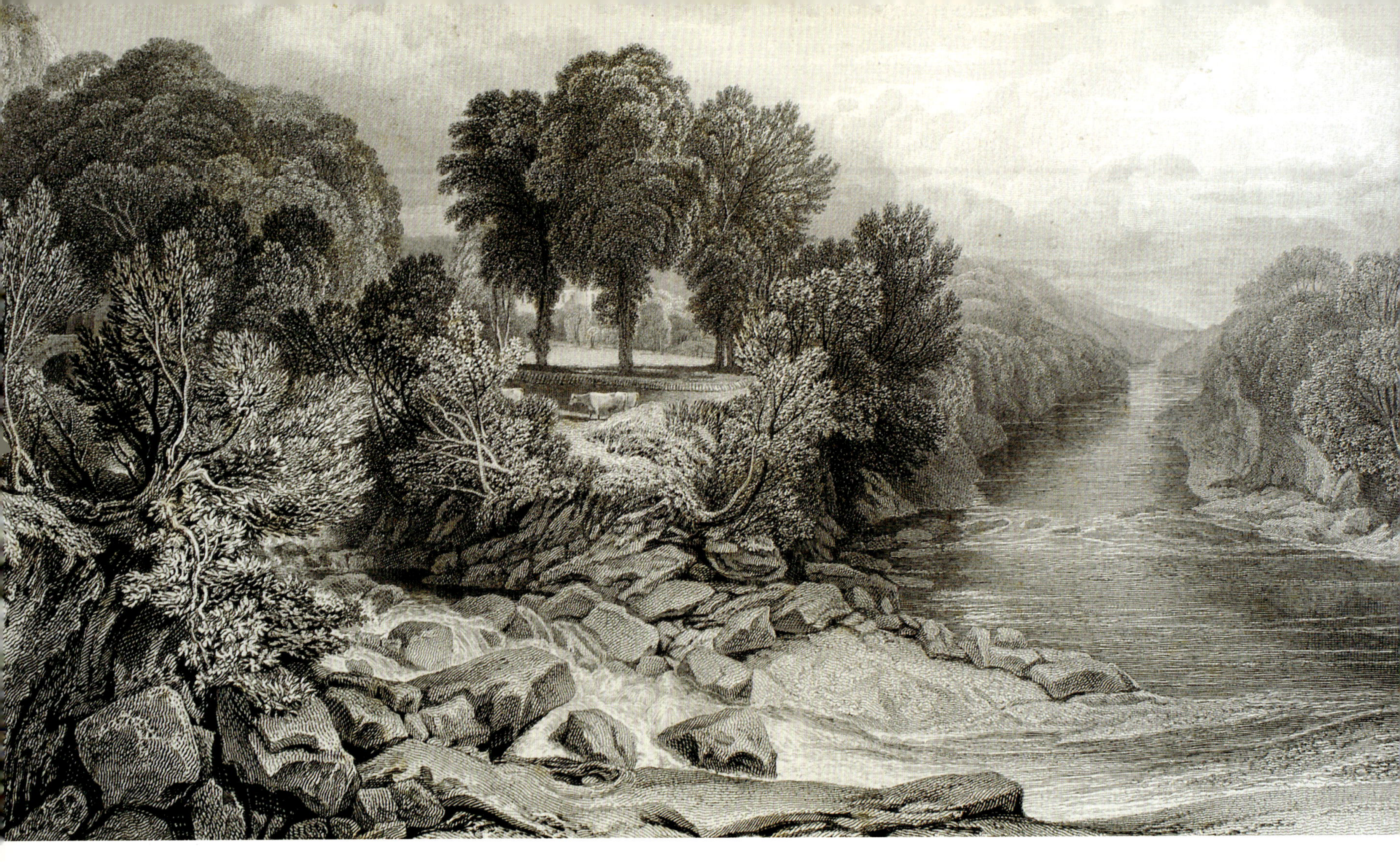

Turner not only lavished great attention on the details of translating his watercolours into engraving, but also immersed himself in the landscape's history. Turner became interested in the folktales that surrounded many of the sights and these fuelled his imagination. According to local myth, the Devil tried to throw the Carlow Stone across Simmer Lake (Semer Water) to Crag End, but it slipped from his grasp and landed at the edge of the lake. Eric Shanes has suggested that Turner includes the marks of the Devil's fingers on the Carlow Stone in the foreground of *Simmer Lake, near Askrigg* (plate 20) and that the horns on the cow to the right of the stone represent the Devil's horns.[12] Turner has continued to emphasise these details in the final engraving.

PLATE 49

Opposite

Detail

John Pye

(1782 – 1874)

Junction of the Greta and the Tees at Rokeby

1819

Engraving after J. M. W. Turner

The Bowes Museum

PLATE 50

Right

Detail

John Pye

(1782 – 1874)

Junction of the Greta and the Tees at Rokeby

1819

Engraving after J. M. W. Turner

The Bowes Museum

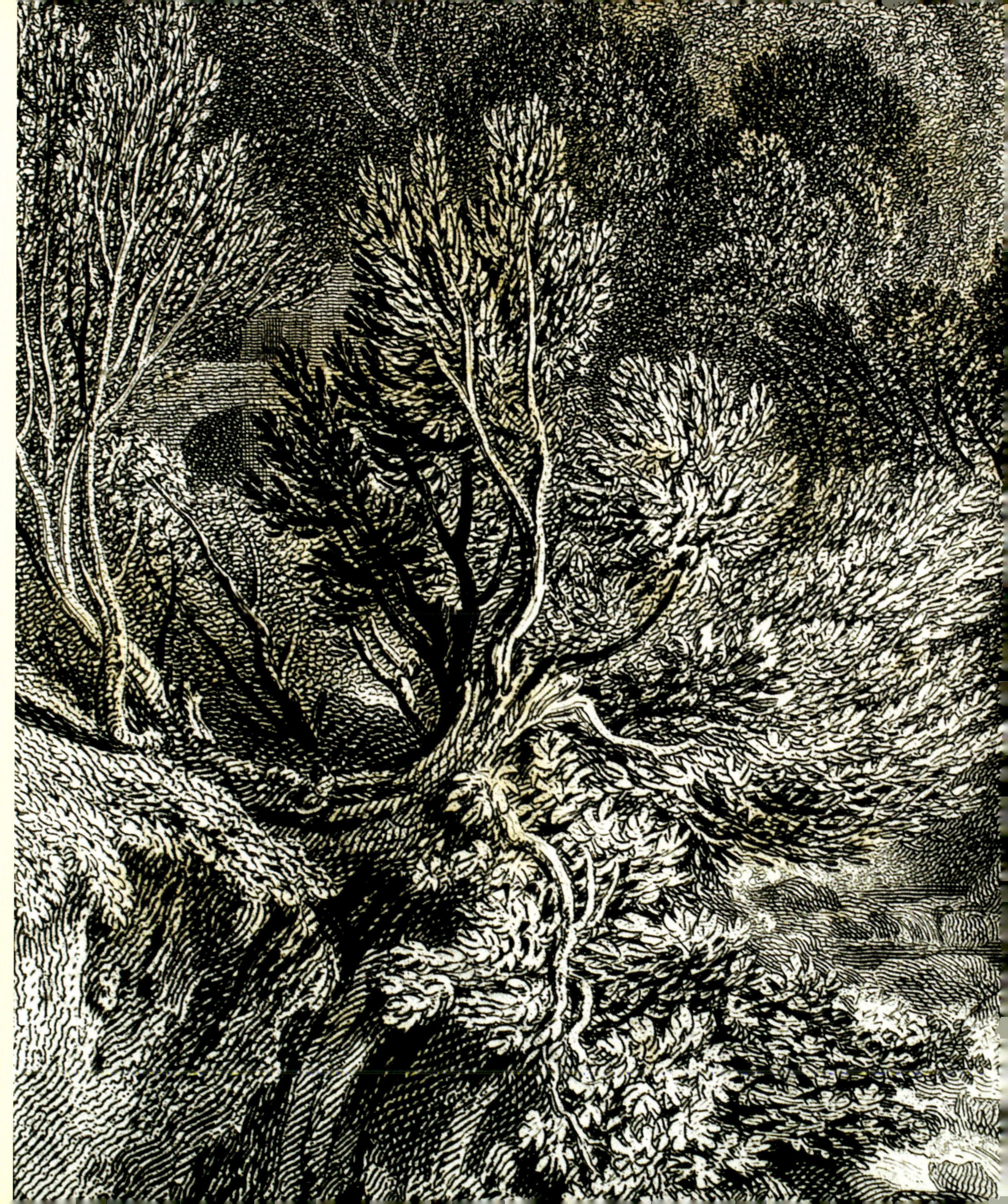

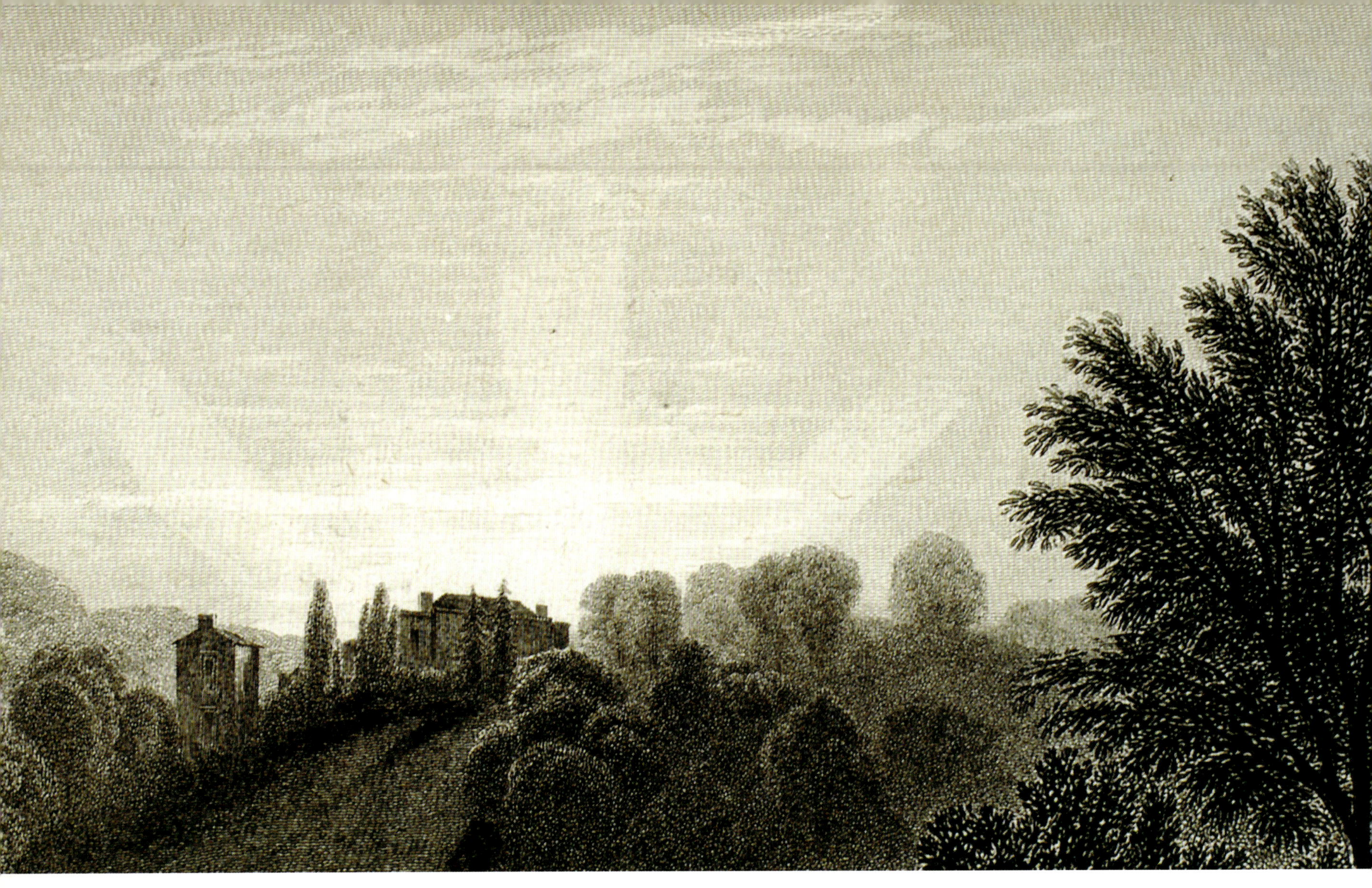

In the engraving of *Wycliffe, near Rokeby* Turner has added beams of sunlight rising from behind Wycliffe Hall (plate 51). Rawlinson states that the engraver John Pye asked Turner why he wished for the sunlight to be added and that he replied, 'That is where Wickliffe was born and the light of the glorious Reformation'.[13] When he questioned further about the geese Turner explained, 'Oh, they are the old superstitions which the genius of reformation is driving away!'[14] It was thought that Wycliffe was the birthplace of John Wycliffe (1324 – 1384). A proof of *Wycliffe, near Rokeby* (plate 52), now in the British Museum, to which Turner added a long inscription outlining Wycliffe's translation of the bible into English and the legislation that prevented its distribution, confirms Turner's meaning behind the beams of sunlight and the geese.[15]

Turner's watercolour of Aske Hall (plate 23) lacks the sheep in the field in front of the Hall, which appear in the engraving. An early engraver's proof is also without sheep, but a later proof in the collection of the British Museum, and later published editions, depict the introduction of two groups of sheep, which have been added for decorative effect.[16] Attention to minute details heightens the drama within the image and enlivens the curiosity of the viewer. It would seem that each image was studied and the addition of no detail was too arduous if it embellished the image as required. For those with access to images of both the watercolour and various states of the engraving there is the opportunity to immerse oneself for hours as slight variations are identified.

The watercolours that Turner produced for publication as engraved images were generally made especially for commissions from authors, poets or publishers. These watercolours were usually then sold soon after the engraved image was finished. Towards the end of his life the watercolours were kept by Turner and merely loaned out to the engraver for a fee. Therefore these watercolours were rarely exhibited and were only known to the public in their printed form. The watercolour *Brignall Church* was destroyed in a fire over one hundred years ago and is now only preserved in the engraved format (plate 27). We can only wonder at the beauty of the watercolour that Ruskin described as 'The perfect image of the painter's mind.'[17]

In the same vein we can only speculate at the exquisite elegance the watercolour *Lancaster Sands* (plate 53) may have taken on as an engraving. It is probable that Turner produced this image for *An History of Richmondshire* before the project was terminated prematurely. The journey across the sands to Lancaster was extremely dangerous due to unpredictable tides, quicksand and fog.[18] Turner depicts strong shafts of light falling from the clouds and reflecting upon the sand, illustrating the beauty and strangeness of the landscape. He also suggests the haste with which coaches had to travel to avoid being caught by the rising tide.

PLATE 51

Opposite

Detail

John Pye

(1782 – 1874)

Wycliffe, near Rokeby

1823

Engraving proof after J. M. W. Turner

The Bowes Museum

PLATE 52

Right

John Pye

(1782 – 1874)

Wycliffe, near Rokeby

Engraving proof after J. M. W. Turner

The British Museum

THE ENGRAVER JOHN PYE ASKED TURNER WHY HE WISHED FOR THE SUNLIGHT TO BE ADDED TO THE ENGRAVING AND HE REPLIED, *'THAT IS WHERE WICKLIFFE WAS BORN AND THE LIGHT OF THE GLORIOUS REFORMATION'.*

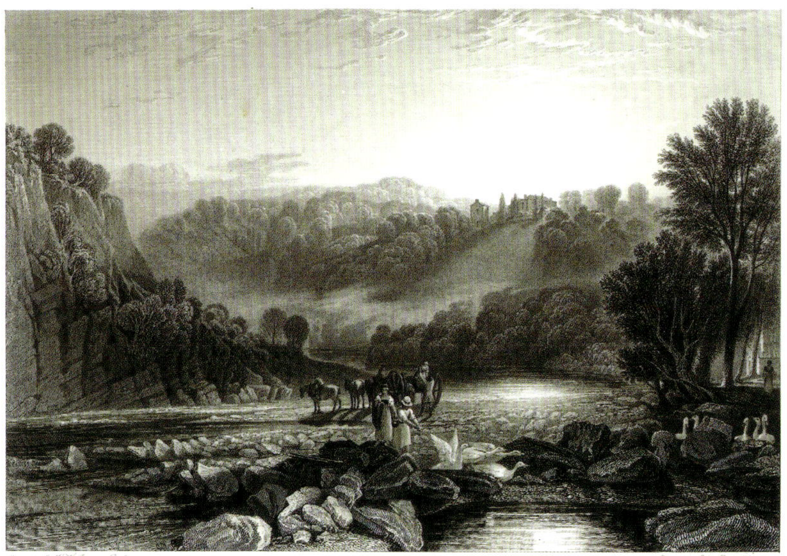

THE BODY OF WORK THAT SURVIVES AFTER Turner in the engraved form is testament to the skills of line engravers. Through their craftsmanship the texture and form of leaves come alive within *Gibside, County Durham*, whilst the intricacies and rough surfaces of the geological rock formations in *Hardraw Fall* are rendered even more perfectly than in Turner's watercolour. Turner and the line engravers that worked alongside him had raised engraving to new heights. The printed image was no longer a mere impression, it had become an art form in itself, embellished and enriched by the hand of the engraver.

Engravers were not included in the founding members of the Royal Academy in 1768. A year later a maximum number of six engravers were admitted as Associate members and were given the privilege of each displaying two prints in the annual exhibition. However, they were not permitted to hold any of the Royal Academy's formal posts. When the Academy introduced the Associate membership for artists who had not yet attained the standards required for full membership the engravers were given the new membership title of Associate Engravers.[19] Whilst Associate members could rise to the status of Academician, engravers could not, making the distinction between fine artist and craftsman explicit. Although in theory up to twelve prints could be shown at each exhibition, rarely more than three prints were displayed annually.[20]

Although Turner did not actively defend the rights of engravers or openly encourage their inclusion within the establishment of the Royal Academy, through the translation of his works into the engraved image a number of engravers emerged whose skills were varied and interpreted an image onto the printed page with precision and brilliance.

Line engraving was seen in the eyes of the Royal Academy as a process of translation rather than an art form and did not warrant full recognition. Without full endorsement from the Academy the line engraver would always remain a craftsman in the eyes of the public rather than attaining the prized status of artist and would continue to lack access to the patronage that would allow him to work more freely as an artist. Line engravers continued to lobby for entry into the Royal Academy as full members. In 1835 a Select Committee was set up to investigate their claim and report to parliament. The following year Longman & Co. printed a pamphlet, annotated by John Pye, one of Turner's most accomplished engravers, outlining the proceedings of the Select Committee. The process was largely unsuccessful and engravers did not gain full membership to the Academy until 1853.[21]

The engravings that were produced after Turner's watercolours of Northern subjects may still be regarded by some as mere replicas of an original. The technical qualities of engraving skilfully render the delicate textures and shading of each watercolour. Turner and his engravers subtly enhanced each image, intensifying shadows, elegantly heightening highlights as well as adding figures and animals to draw the viewer's eye into the image. The intricate details and graceful contours surpass the qualities of a mere reproduction and continue to excite and enthral the viewer.

PLATE 53

Opposite

J. M. W. Turner

Lancaster Sands

Watercolour on paper

Birmingham Museums and Art Gallery

THE JOURNEY ACROSS THE SANDS TO LANCASTER WAS EXTREMELY DANGEROUS DUE TO UNPREDICTABLE TIDES, QUICKSAND AND FOG. TURNER DEPICTS STRONG SHAFTS OF LIGHT FALLING FROM THE CLOUDS AND REFLECTING UPON THE SAND, ILLUSTRATING THE BEAUTY AND STRANGENESS OF THE LANDSCAPE.

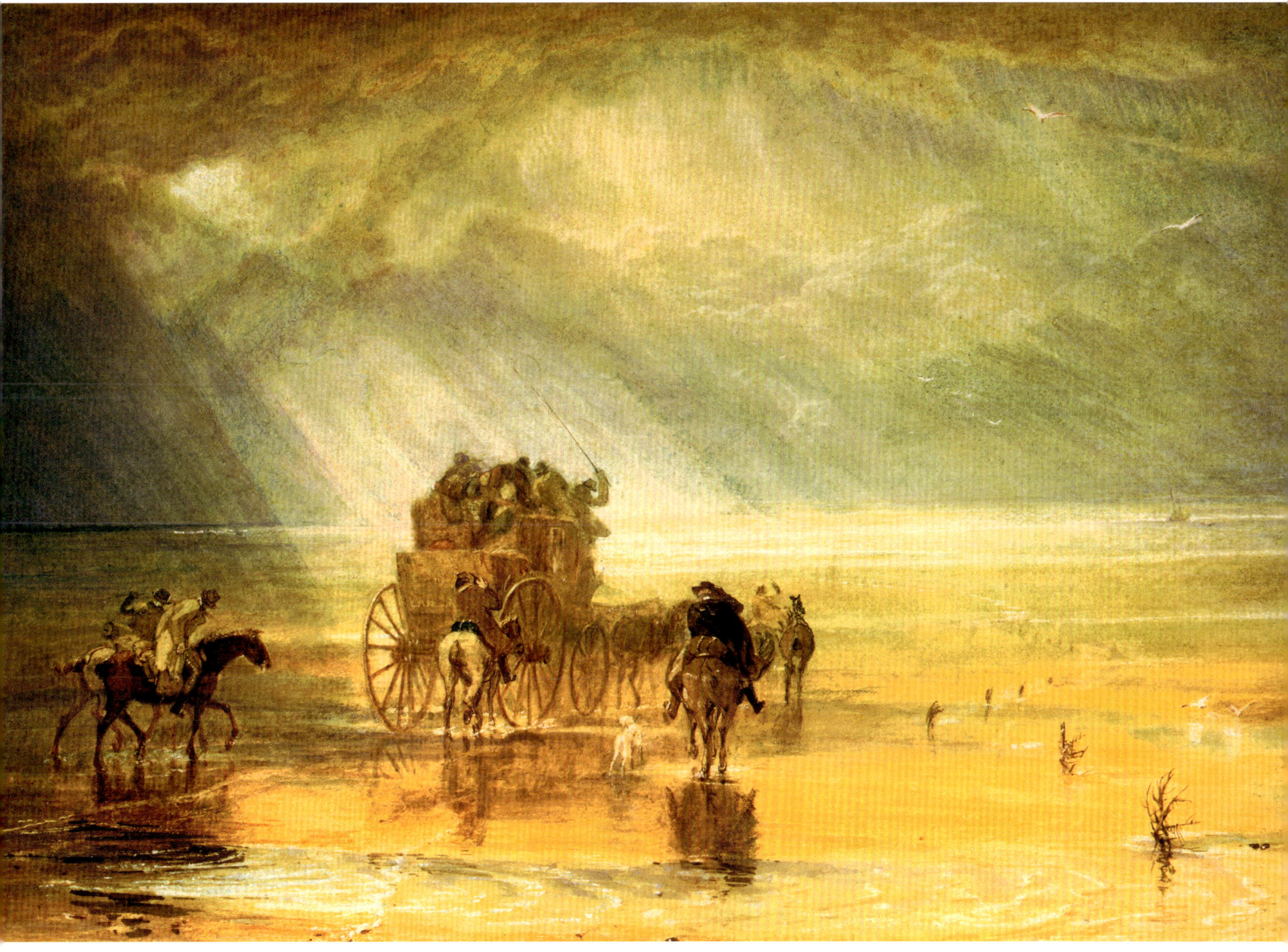

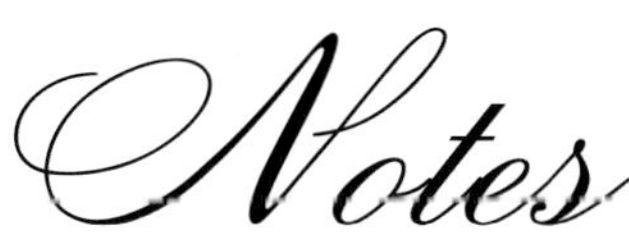

Introduction

1 David Hill, *Harewood Masterpieces; English Watercolours and Drawings* (Oxford: Harewood House Trust, 1995), p. 15.

2 When Turner was commissioned to produce images to illustrate James Hakewill's *Picturesque Tour of Italy*, unable to visit Italy himself, he adapted Hakewill's drawings.

3 Luke Herrmann, *Turner Prints, The Engraved Work of J.M.W Turner* (Oxford: Phaidon, 1990), p. 18.

4 David Hill, *In Turner's Footsteps* (London: John Murray, 1984), pp. 15–16.

5 *Ibid*, p. 15.

6 *Ibid*, p. 16.

7 *Ibid*, p. 18. Turner visited Switzerland and France during the short break in fighting that followed the Peace of Amiens in 1802.

8 David Hill, *Turner in Yorkshire* (York: Ebor Press, 1980), pp. 29–30.

9 David Hill, *In Turner's Footsteps*, p. 18.

10 W. G. Rawlinson, *The Engraved Work of J. M. W. Turner, R.A.* (London: Macmillan, 1908), p. 89.

11 David Hill, *In Turner's Footsteps*, p. 36.

12 W. G. Rawlinson, *The Engraved Work of J. M. W. Turner, R.A.*, p. 89 .

13 David Hill, *In Turner's Footsteps*, p. 25.

14 Anne Lyles and Diane Perkins, *Colour into Line, Turner and the Art of Engraving* (London: Tate, 1989), p. 36.

15 The 10th Earl of Strathmore was father to John Bowes, co-founder of The Bowes Museum. The two watercolours of Gibside were purchased by The Bowes Museum in the 1980s; *Gibside, County Durham, The Seat of the Earl of Strathmore* (1983) and *Gibside from the North* (1985).

16 Reproduced in John Gage, ed., *Collected Correspondence of J. M. W. Turner* (Oxford: Clarendon Press, 1980), p. 71.

17 Robert Surtees, *The History and Antiquities of the County Palatine of Durham* (London: Nichols and Bentley, 1816–1823).

18 *Ibid*.

Retracing Turner's Sketching Tours

1 *Gibside, County Durham, The Seat of the Earl of Strathmore* and *Hardraw Fall* are examples of this practice.

2 Turner combines foreground details from different sketchbooks in both *Aske Hall* and *Barnard Castle*.

3 *St. Agatha's Abbey, Easby*.

4 *Chain Bridge over the Tees*.

5 Details of the Bridge Inn in *Hornby Castle from Tatham Church*; the wall in foreground of *Aske Hall*.

6 References in Roman numerals and accompanying number refer to the sketchbook and page numbers as given by Finberg and still used today. Alexander Joseph Finberg, *A Complete Inventory of the Drawings of the Turner Bequest* (London: H.M.S.O. 1909).

7 Margaret Hunt, *Richmondshire Illustrated by Twenty Line Engravings after Drawings by J.M.W. Turner, R.A. with Descriptions by Mrs. Alfred Hunt* (London: H Virtue & Co. 1891), p. 16. Thomas Dunham Whitaker *An History of Richmondshire* (London: Longman & Co. 1823), opposite p. 113. Labelled on the plan of the abbey 'Old Barn'.

8 Margaret Hunt, *Richmondshire Illustrated*, p. 25.

9 For the dates on which Turner sketched on his Richmondshire tour in 1816, refer to David Hill, *In Turner's Footsteps* (London: John Murray, 1984).

10 CXLV 147a.

11 CXLV 147.

12 Eric Shanes, *Turner's England 1810–38* (London: Cassell, 1990), p. 89. According to local legend, the Devil tried to throw the Carlow Stone across Simmer Lake (Semer Water) to Crag End, but it slipped from his grasp and landed at the edge of the lake. Turner depicts the marks of the Devil's fingers on Carlow Stone in the foreground of his watercolour.

13 CXLV 146a.

14 CXLVII 3a – 4.

15 David Hill, *In Turner's Footsteps* , p. 48. According to local legend, an Angel disguised as a beggar asked for shelter at a number of houses in

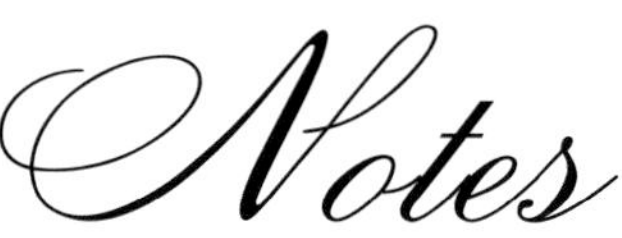

the village on the edge of Simmer Lake (Semer Water). No one in the village would take him in until he came to a run-down dwelling where an old couple lived. Although they were poor, they took him in and fed him with what little they had. In the morning the Angel left their house, summoning the lake to rise up and to flood the whole village, saving only the house of the couple who fed him. The lone house can be seen standing on the edge of the lake in Turner's watercolour.

16 CXLVIII 15a – 28a.

17 See above – *'1797 North of England'*.

18 For example CXLV 108 and CXLVII 24.

19 CXLV 105a.

20 Margaret Hunt, *Richmondshire Illustrated*, p. 74.

21 CXLVII 29 labelled 'Brignall Church' and the less detailed CXLV 106 with the 'Greta' labelled.

22 See above – *'1797 North of England'*.

23 Denis Coggins 'The First Winch Bridge' *The Teesdale Record Society Journal*, Third Series, Vol. 6 (1998), pp. 30–36 .

24 CXLV 80a.

25 CXLV 77a and 78a.

26 Thomas Dunham Whitaker, *An History of Richmondshire*, p. 317.

27 CXLV 77a.

28 Thomas Dunham Whitaker, *An History of Richmondshire*, p. 320 and opposite p. 317.

29 *Ibid*, p. 263.

30 The extension of the sketch on page 42 of Turner's sketchbook was not included in the watercolour.

31 CXLV 63 and 64.

32 Margaret Wills *Gibside and the Bowes Family* (Chichester: Phillimore for Society of Antiquaries of Newcastle upon Tyne, 1995), p. 46.

33 CLVI 13a.

34 For example CLIX 63a and CLVI 14a.

35 CLVI 12a.

A Précis of Turner's Watercolour Materials, Techniques and Ideas

1 A. J. Finberg, *The Life of J. M. W. Turner R.A.* (Oxford: Clarendon Press, 1961), p. 61.

2 *Ibid*, p. 63.

3 W. Shaw Sparrow, in *The Genius of Turner* ed. Holme (London: *The Studio*, 1930), pp. vii–viii. See also Eric Shanes, 'Turner and the Scale Practice in British Watercolour Art', *Apollo*, November (1997), pp. 45–51 and *Turner's Watercolour Explorations* (London: Tate, 1997). See also John Gage, *Colour in Turner; Poetry and Truth* (London: Studio Vista, 1969) p. 32.

4 The crucial effect of tools on style was recognised by C. F. Bell, in his introduction to *A List of the Works Contributed to Public Exhibitions by J. M. W. Turner* (London: George Bell, 1901) where he noted:

It will, perhaps, always remain doubtful whether ill-sized paper or feebly toned pigments were among the causes which contributed originally to the rise of the stained manner, but it is unquestionable that without the great improvements made towards the close of the eighteenth century and early nineteenth century in the manufacture of artists' materials, no such revolution as that which gave birth to modern watercolour art could have been carried through.

5 An in-depth and pioneering survey of the crucial role different papers played on Turner's innovative watercolour style can be found in Peter Bower, *Turner's Papers* (London: Tate, 1990) and *Turner's Later Papers 1820–1851* (London: Tate, 1999).

6 For some excellent research in this area, see: Bronwyn A. Ormsby, Joyce H. Townsend, Brian W. Singer *et al.* 'British Watercolour Cakes from the Eighteenth to the Early Twentieth Century', *Studies in Conservation*, 50 (2005), pp. 45–66. See also Sarah L. Vallance, B. W. Singer, S. M. Hitchen *et al.* 'The Development and Initial Application of a Gas Chromatographic method for the Characterisation of Gum Media', *Journal of the American Institute of Conservation*, (1998), vol. 37, no. 3, pp. 294–311. For more information on J. M. W. Turner's watercolour materials and techniques see: Joyce H. Townsend, 'The Analysis of Watercolour Materials, In Particular Turner's Watercolours at the Tate Gallery, 1790s to 1840s', *The Broad Spectrum* (London: Archetype, 2002), pp. 83–88, and *Turner's Painting Techniques* (London: Tate, 1993).

7 Daniel V. Thompson, in his book *The Materials and Techniques of*

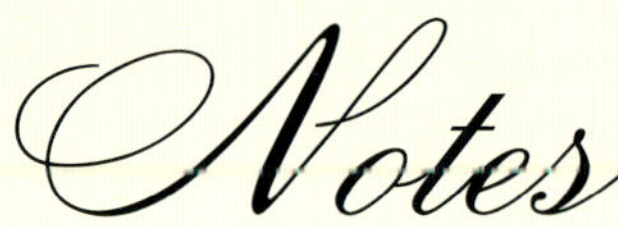

Medieval Painting (New York: Dover, 1956) p. 45 recognised:

Binding media always have a certain influence upon a pigment's behaviour... The transparency of any pigment is affected by the medium which surrounds its particles and by the amount of medium mixed with it.

8 Indeed, throughout history, artists, colourmen and the curious have experimented with a whole range of different substances – gums, resins, egg yolk, egg glair, bone, skin and milk based glues, casein, honey, sugars, oils, waxes, varnishes, soaps, starches, and so on, both singularly and in various combinations known as temperas, emulsions, gumptions and McGuelps, in order to create the most flexible, practical and effective pigment binder for painting images.

9 John Gage, *Colour in Turner; Poetry and Truth* p. 105.

10 John Ruskin, *The Elements of Drawing* (Smith Elder, 1857), pp. 137–160.

11 *Ibid* p. 138.

12 *Turner Studies* (London: Tate), vol.5, no. 2, p. 26.

Turner and the Art *of* Engraving

1 John Ruskin, as quoted in Eric M. Lee, *Translations: Turner and Printmaking* (New Haven: Yale 1993) p. 7.

2 Anne Lyles and Diane Perkins, *Colour into Line, Turner and the Art of Engraving* (London: Tate, 1989), p. 9.

3 Luke Herrmann, *Turner Prints, The Engraved J. M. W. Turner* (Oxford: Phaidon, 1990), p. 9.

4 W. G. Rawlinson, *The Engraved Work of J. M. W. Turner, R.A.* (London: Macmillan, 1908), ix. Luke Herrmann questions this as Turner's introduction to the art of line engraving as Smith worked mainly in mezzotint and stipple engraving.

5 Anne Lyles and Diane Perkins, *Colour into Line, Turner and the Art of Engraving*, p. 21.

6 W. G. Rawlinson, *The Engraved Work of J. M. W. Turner, R.A.* (London: Macmillan, 1908), xii.

7 An early engraver's proof of *St. Agatha's Abbey, Easby* is inscribed *Etch'd by J. le Keux* whilst in the later proof this has changed to *Engraved by J. le Keux.*

8 Anne Lyles and Diane Perkins, *Colour into Line, Turner and the Art of Engraving*, p. 21.

9 Engraved inscription: *Drawn by Turner* and *Etched by S. Middiman* and *Engraved by John Pye.*

10 Rather unusually, the owners of the properties illustrated in Robert Surtees's *The History and Antiquities of the County Palatine of Durham* paid for both the watercolours by Turner and for the engraving plates. The watercolours of Gibside and the engraving plate remained the property of the Earl of Strathmore. Turner destroyed a large number of engraving plates to avoid prints taken from worn plates entering the market place. The plate of *Gibside, County Durham* is one of a small number of plates that remain in their original engraved state.

11 Charles Stokes was Turner's stockbroker and assembled one of the finest examples of Turner's *Liber Studiorum*. His collection of prints after Turner and engraver's proofs indicates a contemporary interest in the process of production and an admiration of the engraver's skills.

12 Eric Shanes, *Turner's England 1810–38* (London: Cassell, 1990), p. 89.

13 W. G. Rawlinson, *The Engraved Work of J. M. W. Turner, R.A.*, p. 98.

14 *Ibid*, p. 98.

15 Eric Shanes, *Turner's England 1810–38*, pp. 86–87. The full inscription is transcribed in Appendix II in James Hamilton, *Turner's Britain* (London: Merrell, 2003), p. 196.

16 W. G. Rawlinson, *The Engraved Work of J. M. W. Turner, R.A.*, p. 93.

17 Quoted in David Hill, *Turner in Yorkshire* (York: Ebor Press, 1980), p. 82.

18 *Ibid*, pp. 84–85.

19 Sarah Hyde, 'Printmakers and the Royal Academy Exhibitions, 1780–1836', in *Art on the Line*, ed. David H. Solkin (New Haven: Yale University Press, 2001), pp. 217–228 (p. 217).

20 *Ibid*, p. 218.

21 *Ibid*, p. 228.